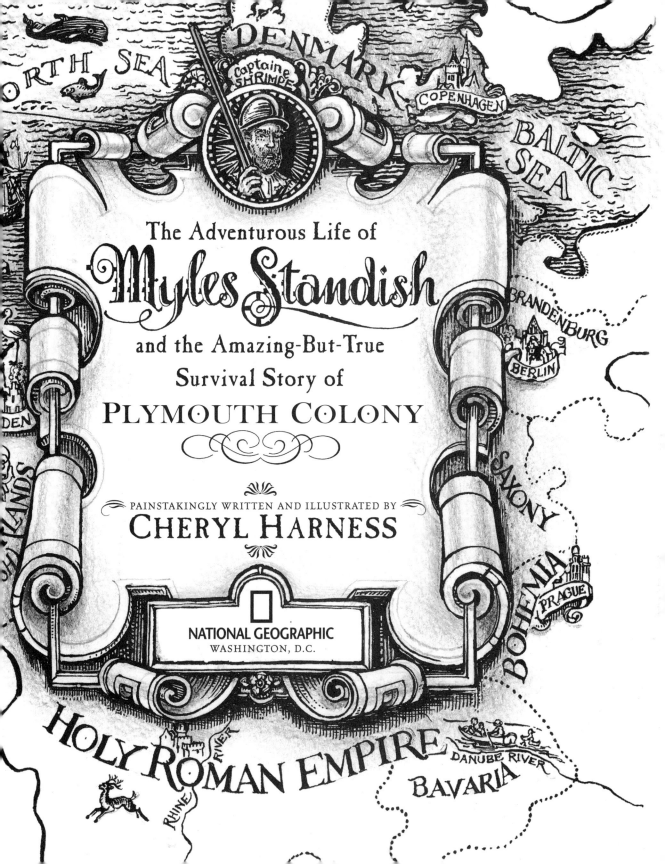

The Adventurous Life of

Myles Standish

and the Amazing-But-True
Survival Story of
PLYMOUTH COLONY

PAINSTAKINGLY WRITTEN AND ILLUSTRATED BY

CHERYL HARNESS

NATIONAL GEOGRAPHIC
WASHINGTON, D.C.

From my years young in days of youth,
God did make known to me his truth,
and call'd me from my native place
For to enjoy the means of grace.
In wilderness he did me guide,
And in strange lands for me provide.
In fears and wants;
    through weal and woe,
       A Pilgrim passed I to and fro.

     — Governor William Bradford
     Colony of New Plymouth

Contents

*T*HE 102 MEN, WOMEN, AND CHILDREN who set out to cross the Atlantic Ocean on September 6, 1620, prayed for God's protection in the New World. As an extra precaution they brought along a one-man army, Captain Myles Standish.

We don't know exactly at what time-space intersection Myles came into the world. Most likely he was born in 1584, perhaps in the village of Chorley, in Lancashire, England. There are Standishes there from way back; their family crest sports an owl with a rat in its talons. Others claim that he was born in Ellanbane, on the Isle of Man in the Irish Sea. From book to book his first name is spelled Myles, the old-fashioned way, or the modernized Miles. Either way, it comes from a Latin word: *miles*. It means "soldier." His parents named him well, for a soldier is definitely what their son turned out to be.

Here in Myles's unimaginable future, we know something about how he looked and acted. He was short, tough, and when he got mad, which was often, his face turned as red as his hair. These things earned him a nickname: "Captaine Shrimpe." His actions earned him a place of honor in the story of Plymouth Colony. Time and again, those colonial pioneers found a steadfast friend in Myles Standish. There, at the edge of the American wilderness, such friendship was a matter of life and death.

ARCTIC OCEAN

SIBERIA

ASIA

NORTH AMERICA

MONGOLIA

MANCHURIA

KOREA

JAPAN

MING EMPIRE
CHINA

BURMA

ANNAM

SIAM

CAMBODIA

BORNEO

PHILIPPINE
ISLANDS
(Spanish)

SPICE
ISLANDS (Port.)

PACIFIC OCEAN

Sir FRANCIS DRAKE sails around the world. 1577~1580

EQUATOR

AUSTRALIA

"All the world's a
stage, and all the
men and women
merely players..."
Wm. Shakespeare
1564-1616

When
MYLES STANDISH
came into the world
c. 1600

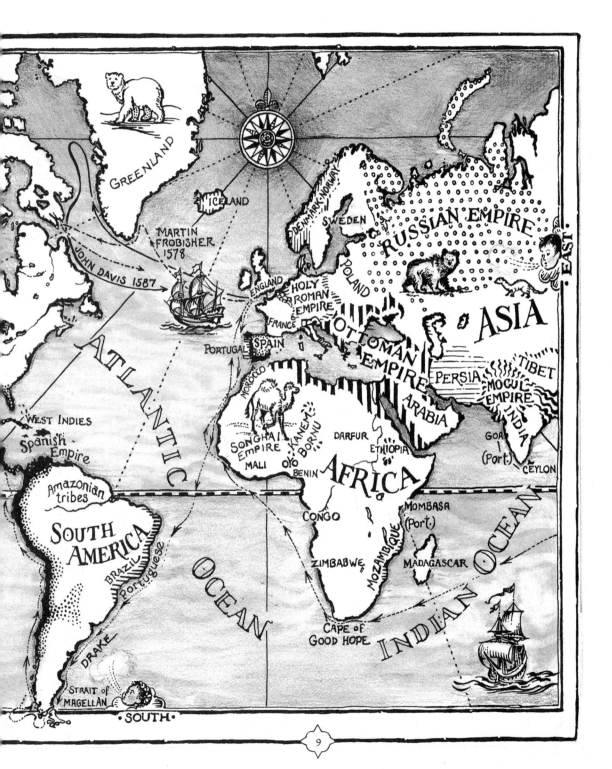

Life along the River Thames in the time of Good Queen Bess

CHAPTER ONE

Thrones, Steeples, & Changing Peoples

MYLES STANDISH, ELIZABETHAN

*

THE RENAISSANCE, A TIME OF GREAT ART and learning, was coming to an end. For nearly a century before Myles Standish was born, in 1584 most likely, explorers from Europe had been sailing on seas, treasure-questing and colonizing in lands far, far away from their home ports. Thanks to them, Europeans were getting to know tobacco and that other New World curiosity, the potato. Barbary *corsairs* (fierce pirates) were terrorizing square-rigged ships and galleons on the Mediterranean Sea.

Art of the highest quality was being made in the African kingdom of Benin, in Ming Dynasty China, and in Spain by a

---

1584   Note: The time line features events that took place around the world during Myles's lifetime.

In Russia's far north, a seaport is founded. Arkangelsk (Archangel) is frozen much of the year.

IVAN IV

March 18 –
Ivan the Terrible *is dead. Thanks to him, many a Russian had died, including his own son and heir. Now Ivan's younger son,* **Fyodor,** *takes the throne, but watch out for the new czar's ruthless brother-in-law,* **Boris Gudunov** *(see 1591 & 1598).*

great painter called El Greco. Russia's first *czar* (emperor), the murderous Ivan IV, was on his deathbed. Portuguese traders were shipping boatloads of Africans into slavery in Europe and beyond, while in Denmark astronomer Tycho Brahe was mapping the stars. More, more, and more of the islanders of Indonesia were adopting the religion of Islam.

Walter Ralegh* had claimed and named a vast chunk of eastern America Virginia, in honor of England's "Virgin Queen," the never-married Queen Elizabeth I. As of 1584, she had been on the throne for 26 years. This meant that Captain Standish and the other men and women aboard the *Mayflower* had grown up in the Elizabethan Age, a golden era in the history of England when their island nation was rich, energetic, adventurous, and optimistic. Most important, during Elizabeth's reign, she and her subjects were slightly more willing to live and let live when it came to matters of religion. It hadn't been like that for many years before the Elizabethan Age, and it certainly wasn't the case after "Good Queen Bess" died. Then her cousin James took the throne, and the King James version of England was pretty stormy.

*Current studies indicate that Sir Walter spelled his name without the "i."

1584

July 10 –
William the Silent, *prince of Orange, who'd campaigned for Dutch freedom from Spain, is murdered, thanks to the active encouragement of the Spanish King* **Philip II**.

William Baffin, *future explorer, is born in England (see 1616).*

Writer **William Shakespeare** *and scientist* **Galileo Galilei** *turn 20 years old.*

Harsh but lively was life in Myles's England.

The new king treated some of his subjects so badly, on account of their religious views, that they had to leave their homeland. It was some of these people who ended up aboard the *Mayflower*. In order to understand these colonial pioneers and their shipmate, Captain Standish, you have to know a little bit more about what had been going on in England and the rest of Europe in the long years before they ever got on the boat.

When Myles was little, there were plenty of old folks around who remembered the monarchs before Elizabeth: her sister Queen Mary I, her brother King Edward VI, and even their dad, King Henry VIII. Even if he hadn't had six queens one after another, he'd be pretty hard to forget. The reigns of

1585

In France, another brutal, religious civil war breaks out, the **War of the Three Henrys**, between supporters of **Henry of Guisse, King Henry III** (both Catholic), and Protestant Prince **Henry of Navarre**.

Walter Ralegh sends 108 men to establish a colony on Roanoke Island, near present-day North Carolina.

The great poet of France **Pierre de Ronsard** dies. So does Pope **Gregory XIII**. He's replaced by **Pope Sixtus V**.

Henry Tudor (the king's family name) and his children were very much a part of the titanic storm of ideas known as the Reformation. Know about the Reformation, and you'll know why Myles's companions aboard the *Mayflower* were so desperate to put an ocean between themselves and Europe.

THE REFORMATION

*

EUROPEANS IN THE EARLY 1500s would tell you that the main religion was Christianity, and when they spoke of the Church, they meant the Catholic Church based in Rome. On October 31, 1517, this began to change. That's when a German priest named Martin Luther officially objected to the way the Church did its work of guarding people's relationships with God. Martin thought that the Church should be reformed. His protest was like a great, big rock tossed into a pond, sending out

---

1585

1586

Queen Elizabeth I *sends an army to help the Dutch fight off their Spanish rulers.*

Dutch mathematician and engineer **Simon Stevin** *introduces the decimal system.*

Wise **Akbar,** *the grandson of the great* **Babur,** *adds the kingdom of Kashmir to his Muslim Mogul Empire, which stretches from Persia through India to the Bay of Bengal.*

rippling waves in all directions. His act touched off the Reformation, a mighty argument about the nature of God and what a Christian must do and believe if his or her soul was to wind up safely in heaven. For more than a hundred years, this shock wave of ideas sparked religious civil wars, split the Church apart, and affected the lives of millions of people in Europe and the Americas.

The Reformation was fueled and supercharged by the earlier inventions of moveable type and printing presses. As more words were printed, more folks learned to read them, and by 1500, more than a thousand print shops were scattered around Europe. When Martin Luther translated the Bible from Latin into German and had it printed, ordinary folks could finally read the Holy Scriptures for themselves. Revolutionary!

More and more people were learning the printing crafts.

Sir Francis Drake's *men attack Spanish settlements on Hispaniola, in Florida, and along the Spanish Main (pirates' nickname for South America's northern coast). Potatoes from Peru are just part of Drake's New World loot. He gives the Roanoke colonists a lift home to England. They'd had it with America.*

A plot to kill **Queen Elizabeth I** *is discovered. Her cousin* **Mary, Queen of Scots,** *is rumored to be involved.*

LUTHERAN

CALVINIST and LUTHERAN

ANGLICAN (Church of ENGLAND)

CALVINIST and or HUGUENOT

Eastern ORTHODOX (Christian)

CATHOLIC

MUSLIM

mixed: Calvinist, Catholic, & Lutheran

Myles Standish's boyhood was a time of powerful monarchs, such as Philip II of Spain. He and the Holy Roman Emperor Rudolph II were part of the Habsburg dynasty. Kings and queens sent many a brave sailor to find faraway riches—too bad for folks already living in the New World, where smallpox, measles, and other European diseases wiped out multitudes.

Plague epidemics made dreadful dents in Europe's population. Cities stank, dentistry was frightful, and justice was fierce. From the 1500s into the 1700s, tens of thousands of heretics and witches (these, mostly women) were tortured and executed. Times were hard, but they were enlightened with learning and idealism, singing, dancing, feasting and fashion, and exploration.

As lines were drawn between Protestants and Catholics, their troubles grew and grew until they exploded in the disastrous Thirty Years' War in 1618, two years before grownup Myles Standish left England for America.

Because once they did that, people came up with all sorts of ideas on their own about what God wanted. Once they had access to paper, ink, and a printing press, they could spread their radical thoughts all over the place!

All across Europe, Christians who took the same ideas to heart, more or less, began getting together to worship and study. These gatherings of believers were the beginnings of churches called Protestant: They protested the traditional truths taught by the priests and bishops of the Catholic Church. Groups became known by their specific beliefs. For instance, Protestants who wished to purify the Church were called Puritans. Others took on the names of the men whose ideas they followed, such as Martin Luther (Lutherans) and John Calvin (Calvinists). Some of the future Pilgrims of Plymouth were originally called Brownists because they followed the teachings of Robert Browne, one of many Separatists who wanted to separate from the Church.

All of this deep thinking and talking about the life of the spirit made this a very exciting time to be alive. It was something else, too: very, very dangerous. Powerful people did not want the

1587

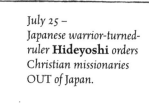

February 8 –
Mary Stuart, Queen of Scots, *is beheaded.*

July 25 –
Japanese warrior-turned-ruler **Hideyoshi** *orders Christian missionaries OUT of Japan.*

King Nanda Bayin *of Burma invades Siam (Thailand).*

I'M HENRY THE 8TH, I AM

*P*opular, powerful King Henry VIII of England planned ahead. He very badly wanted a prince to take over his job after he died, but all he had was a princess. A woman ruling over England? What a nutty idea — just plain wrong! The king figured (a) God put him on the throne to look after England; (b) What Henry wanted (a son) must be God's will for England; (c) God must want the king to do what he had to do to get a son. Out of the dreadful clash of wills between the pope, the king, his wife Queen Catherine of *Aragon* (she came from that kingdom in Spain), and his ministers and advisers came England's break with the Church of Rome. From his new wife Anne Boleyn, the king got another princess: Elizabeth.

Queen Anne's head was chopped off after Henry accused her of bad behavior. Jane Seymour (Queen No. 3) died soon after she had baby Edward. The king divorced Anne of Cleves (Queen No. 4) and had Catherine Howard (Queen No. 5) beheaded. Catherine Parr (Queen No. 6) outlived old Henry VIII. When he died, his young son Edward took the throne, followed by Mary. Then in 1558, their half-sister Elizabeth began her 45-year reign as one of England's greatest monarchs ever.

New settlers come to Roanoke Island. On August 18, **Virginia Dare**, the first American-born English child, comes into the world.

In Africa, Zimba warriors attack the rich city state of Kilwa, on the eastern edge of present-day Tanzania.

The long reign of **Abbas I** begins, a time of greatness for Persia (modern-day Iran). He turns his new capital, Isfahan, into a treasure city of mosques and palaces.

ordinary masses of folks choosing their own religions. What would they choose next? Their kings? Plenty of thoughtful people said their prayers and genuinely believed that folks who went against the Church were *heretics* (people who'd sinned against the true teachings of God.) The Church launched a cruel, deadly campaign, known as the Inquisition, against such sinners. If the Church officials decided that you were a heretic, then not only were you in danger, body and soul, your government would see you as an outlaw. Separation of Church and State? No such thing. How about understanding and tolerance for people with different beliefs? Well, in all of their history, human beings aren't famous for those attitudes.

In the years of the Reformation, in most of the nations of Europe, thousands upon thousands of people were jailed and treated badly, and many a person was cruelly executed. Consider the fate of William Tyndale, who was tied to a stake and set on fire in October of 1536. Why? Not only had he translated the New Testament of the Bible into English and had it printed and smuggled into England, he'd also objected to the way the King of England was treating his queen.

1588

A *time of terrible famine throughout China; people are going hungry.*

English *playwright* **Christopher Marlowe** *writes* The Tragical History of Doctor Faustus, *about a real-life, legendary German magician, who was said to have sold his soul to the devil.*

Thomas Cavendish *becomes the second Englishman — after* **Francis Drake** *— to sail around the world, a feat only barely first accomplished by Italian* **Sebastian del Cano** *back in 1522. Cavendish's boss,* **Ferdinand Magellan,** *died on that awful voyage.*

KING VERSUS POPE

THE SON-STARVED KING OF ENGLAND set his heart on getting a new wife, one who might give birth to a boy, but could Henry VIII, a Catholic king, divorce his lawful queen? No. Would head of the Church Pope Clement VII *annul* (cancel) the royal marriage? Absolutely not.

What was the big deal about this king's marriage problems? They were smack in the middle of a long, painful, even deadly international argument about power: where it came from, and who had it. Most people, including Henry, believed that God gave kings, queens, czars, and emperors the divine right to rule their lands and people with absolute power. This belief was directly connected to the idea that the royal monarch's subjects must share their ruler's religion. It led to the creation of the Anglican Church of England, which was

1589

September 15 –
King Philip II *hoped to invade England with the help of his "invincible" Spanish Armada, but no. It is defeated by storms and nifty English sailing.*

January 5 –
Queen Catherine de Medici *dies. Through her three sons, all kings, she'd ruled over France - fiercely. At her urging, some 50,000 French Protestants were killed back in 1572 in the St. Bartholomew's Day Massacre.*

like the Catholic Church with one big difference: Whoever sat on England's throne was the head of it. No longer could the Pope stop stubborn Henry from divorcing his wife and marrying any lady who caught His Majesty's eye.

So what happened when people's ideas changed, as they did in the Reformation? What happened when they and their ruler believed differently? Trouble. English folks not only had to support the state Church of England with their taxes, they were also expected to show up there on Sunday mornings. It was the law.

Folks with Protestant beliefs were jailed and *persecuted* (treated badly) when Henry VIII was king, because they didn't go along with every single thing taught by England's official church. Catholics in particular had a tough time with Henry as well as with the next king, young Edward VI. When his older half-sister, Mary (Catherine of Aragon's daughter), became the next ruler, this Catholic queen sent nearly 300 Protestants to burn at the stake, earning for herself a dreadful nickname: "Bloody Mary." The weary English people must surely have wondered what would happen when the queen's young half-sister took the throne. How would Elizabeth rule?

1589

1590

English clergyman **William Lee** *invents a machine that knits stockings.*

August 2 – French **King Henry III** *is stabbed to death by a fanatic monk. Soon,* **Henry of Navarre** *takes the throne, but not without a lot more trouble and death in France, long troubled with religious wars.*

William Bradford, *future Pilgrim, is born in Austerfield, England.*

Zacharias Janssen, *a Dutch lens grinder, invents the compound microscope.*

THE GOLDEN AGE OF ELIZABETH

✳

PEACE WAS MORE IMPORTANT TO QUEEN ELIZABETH I than hard, definite religious views. True, those few of her subjects who dared to oppose the state Church of England (questioning her divine authority) faced harsh punishment. More than one Separatist was hanged. Elizabeth, like her dad, was an absolute monarch, but compared to her big sister Mary, the new queen was pretty tolerant. She decided that the state church would be like herself: Protestant, but not extremely so. It would keep some Catholic beliefs and practices. And unlike Mary, strong, clever Elizabeth avoided getting too involved in the awful religious wars being fought on the continent of Europe.

While she was on the throne, England grew rich and famous. Famous for its writers such as William Shakespeare

1591

The Turks, led by Sultan **Murad III**, and the Persians, led by Shah **Abbas I**, end 12 years of fighting.

John White returns to Roanoke Island from a trip to England to find that all of the colonists have disappeared, including his little granddaughter, **Virginia Dare**. To this very day, the Lost Colony of Roanoke remains a mystery.

Italians by the thousands are dying of bubonic plague. For centuries, fleas and rats have been carrying this Black Death all over Europe, Asia, and Africa, and they'll keep right on doing it.

and for its *sea dogs* (sea captains), such as Jack Hawkins and Walter Ralegh. Only a few years before Myles Standish came into the world, Francis Drake sailed all the way around it. Drake, one of the most famous buccaneers and feared pirates of the Elizabethan Age, was fond of capturing Spanish ships and sharing with "Good Queen Bess" the gold, silver, and jewels they carried.

This made King Philip II of Spain more upset than he was already with Queen Elizabeth. He'd married her sister because both he and Queen Mary wanted their nations to be as devoutly Catholic as they were. Then, when Mary died, Philip asked his sister-in-law to marry him, an offer Elizabeth accepted from no one. He did do a couple of things that interested Elizabeth, though. For one thing, his harsh control of the Netherlands led her to send an army there to help the Dutch Protestants. And it was Philip's attempt to invade England that gave Elizabeth and her royal navy a glorious victory against his fleet of warships: the Spanish Armada. That happened in the summer of 1588, when Myles Standish was only about four years old.

1591

Future religious leader **Ann Marbury (Hutchinson)** is born in Lincolnshire, England (see 1643).

May 15 – **Dimitri**, *the 9-year-old son of dead* **Czar Ivan IV**, *is murdered. Was* **Boris Godunov** *trying to guard his power behind Russia's throne? It seems so (see 1605).*

Hunger, fighting, and Portuguese slave traders ravage Africans in the land that is today's still troubled Angola.

SOLDIER MYLES

✳

THE STORIES THAT SURVIVE the hundreds of years since Myles was young say that he was an orphan and that he might well have become a drummer boy. Perhaps that is how he began his military career. He definitely was one of the English soldiers who went to help the Dutch fight off the Spanish.

Warfare always has been dreadful. Whether warriors fought for or against Alexander the Great in ancient times or the American North or South in the 1800s, or, at this writing, for the sake of a democratic Iraqi nation, soldiers face homesickness, boredom, terror, crummy food, and all sorts of discomfort on top of the constant possibility of being wounded or killed. That's how it must have been for Myles. No wonder he was so tough! He probably marched and marched (no trucks, no jeeps) wearing padded *round hose* (breeches, a.k.a. slops) and

French mathematician **François Viete,** *the "father of algebra," has the idea of using letters to represent unknown numbers.*

The citizens of Venice are able to cross their Grand Canal, from the island of Rialto over to the island of San Marco, by way of the newly completed Rialto Bridge.

a *jerkin* (padded vest, perhaps reinforced with little steel plates) over his linen shirt and *doublet* (jacket). He would have worn a *gorget*, too, a curved steel plate to protect his throat. On his head, Myles probably wore a Morion helmet. Its brimmed style was borrowed from the Moors, Arabs from Africa who'd invaded Spain back in the 700s.

The equipment that Captain Standish brought with him to America gives us some idea of what fighting was like in Europe at the turn of the 16th and 17th centuries. Besides helmets, heavy swords, *corselets* (breastplates), and long, heavy, matchlock muskets — more about those later — for the other men, Myles had his elegant *rapier* [RAY-pee-yer], a narrow, two-edged sword, and a more modern flintlock musket.

A temporary *truce* (a cease-fire) was made between the Dutch and the Spanish in 1609, so Myles Standish and the English Army were able to return home. Myles would have been about 25 years old. The *Mayflower* wouldn't be leaving for another 11 years. What did Myles do, beside marry a lady named Rose? Nobody nowadays knows. The dead take their secrets with them. The Standishes don't show up in written records until 1620. Could Myles have met his future shipmates,

1592

Pompeii, Italy — Ruins are discovered of the city destroyed when the volcano Mt. Vesuvius blew its top on August 24, A. D. 79.

For the next six years, a Japanese army of 300,000 men will try to take over Korea where **Admiral Yi-sun-sin** has a powerful new weapon: a warship covered with plates of iron!

The Sultan of Morocco sends an army of 4,000 men and 8,000 camels across the sands of the Sahara into the lands of the **Songhai** on a futile quest for gold.

those religious refugees, when he was in Holland? After all, they'd gone there too, to escape another angry king.

THE QUEEN IS DEAD.
LONG LIVE THE KING.

*

SPRING 1603. QUEEN ELIZABETH I was dead, and England was once again ruled by a king. Sixteen years after Queen Elizabeth had his mother, Mary, Queen of Scots, beheaded (because she'd been in the middle of way too many schemes to swipe Elizabeth's throne), James VI of Scotland became England's absolute monarch, King James I.

Unlike his mother, James was a Protestant. And he was something of a blockhead, said to be "the wisest fool in Christendom." For people who went against the twin powers of English Church and Crown, he cut no slack. He treated

1593

September 13 –
In France, **Michel Eyquem de Montaigne**, well-known for his wise essays about life, is dead.

Italian scientist **Galileo** invents the thermometer. He moves to the University of Padua from Pisa, where he's said to have dropped objects of different weights from the top of the town's Leaning Tower so he could see if they fall at the same speed. They do.

An epidemic of the Black Death closes the doors of London theaters. People are afraid of getting sick.

Truth-seekers flocked to hear earnest preachers.

1594

English playwright **Christopher Marlowe**, 29, dies in a fight in a tavern.

Spaniards hoping to find gold in the land that will be known as Kansas are killed by native warriors.

King Henry IV becomes a Catholic, and the gates of Paris are finally opened to him, king of all France.

Chinese folks are introduced to the sweet potato.

Catholics so badly that one of them, Guy Fawkes, tried to blow him up along with the entire *Parliament* (England's law-making body) in 1605. As for the rebellious Puritans and Separatists who craved a purer, more personal religion than they found in the teachings of the Church of England, "I will make them conform or I will harry them out of the land," said King James, "or else do worse."

The king made good on his promise. This is how William Bradford, future governor and historian of Plymouth Colony, described the treatment his fellow Separatists got: "Sometimes by bloody death and cruel torments; other whiles imprisonments, *banishments* (being sent away) and other hard usages." Such persecution and ugly dealings with state churches is what made the the founders of the United States of America, 170 years away in the misty future, so determined to keep the worship of God separate from matters of government. Such royal persecution made William and his friends all the more determined to worship as they saw fit. But if they were going to do that, these country folk would have to, in William's words, "leave their native soil and country, their lands and livings, and all their friends and familiar acquaintance."

1595

Three deaths: English explorer **Martin Frobisher**, *Dutch geographer/mapmaker* **Gerard Mercator**, *and Italian painter* **Tintoretto**.

Londoners return to the theater to see **William Shakespeare's** Romeo and Juliet *and A* Midsummer Night's Dream.

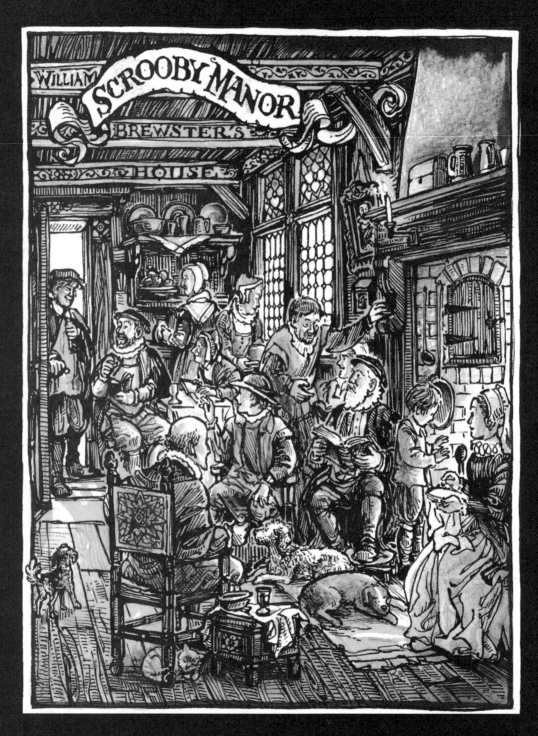

Many a royal guest spent a night or two at the old brick-and-timber Scrooby Manor.

CHAPTER TWO

Pilgrims on the Earth

TWO WILLIAMS

*

T HEY WOULD HAVE TO BECOME *PILGRIMS* (wayfarers, those who went on journeys to foreign lands). Much later on, in the summer of 1620, William himself would use the term. It came from the Bible: "...they were strangers and pilgrims on the earth." (Hebrews 11:13) Much, much later on, some folks capitalized the word. Pilgrims came to mean those who began the colony known as Plymouth. To learn about them, the best place to start would be with a friendship and a lonely teenager's quest for spiritual truth.

William Bradford, who was about six years younger than Myles Standish, lived a little ways from the village of Scrooby,

---

1595

In northern Ireland, **Hugh O'Neill,** the Catholic Earle of Tyrone, leads a rebellion against the Protestant English.

In America, in the household of the leader of the Powhatan people, a daughter is born: **Matoaka,** better known to us by her nickname, **Pocahontas.**

North of Australia, the Dutch begin colonizing the East Indies.

north of Sherwood Forest, legendary home of Robin Hood. He was born in 1590 and named after his father, a Yorkshire farmer. When his dad died and his mom remarried, William got dumped on relatives. The lonely, sickly boy became a passionate Bible reader. He went to prayer-and-preaching meetings and found a mentor, who loaned him books and shared his religious ideals. Eventually, teenage William and 40-something William Brewster worshiped in the older man's house, Scrooby Manor, with Mrs. Brewster, a bunch of like-minded seekers, their white-bearded pastor, Reverend Richard Clyfton, and their teacher, Reverend John Robinson. The two Williams would be friends for nearly 40 years.

William Brewster was a royal postmaster, a job he lost when the authorities found out that he was a Brownist, an admirer of Separatist preacher Reverend Robert Troublechurch Browne. Besides those who'd died in jail, six Brownists had been put to death. The Brewster family, 17-year-old William Bradford, and their friends had little choice but to flee the country.

An English congregation of religious refugees was already established over in the Dutch city of Amsterdam. So, the Scrooby flock had a destination. But what do you do if your government

1596

January –
Sir Francis Drake dies and his body is buried in the Caribbean Sea.

Sir John Harington, poet and godson of **Queen Elizabeth,** invents a "privie of perfection," otherwise known as a flush toilet.

The English begin to know about tomatoes. They admire the plant but they're afraid that these "love apples" might be poisonous.

is mad at you? If it doesn't want you, but won't let you go? How do you sell everything, get the normal travel permissions, get yourselves across a pretty much roadless country to the coast, and hire a boat in a land full of spies who can get money by turning you in? It took two hard tries before William Bradford and his friends (about 25 in all) got out of England. They were cheated, betrayed, robbed, thrown in jail, and even tossed about in a terrifying storm in the North Sea before they finally made it to Amsterdam in 1608. "...They all got over at length," Bradford wrote later on, "some at one time and some at another, and met together again according to their desires, with no small rejoicing."

In the Low Country

✳

MOST OF FLAT, LOW-LYING HOLLAND, the western provinces of the Netherlands, was and is constantly protected by dikes, which hold

1597

François Zaburu *builds the world's first factory ship so he and his whalers can boil the oil from whale blubber while they're out at sea.*

Hideyoshi, *Japan's ruler, fearful of European influences on his country's culture, orders the crucifixion of 26 Christians.*

June 20 – Dutch navigator/ explorer **William Barents** *freezes to death in the Arctic.*

out the surrounding sea. Many a road through the cities and fields of Holland was a *canal* (man-made stream). All kinds of boats were rowed, pulled, and sailed along these light-reflecting waterways, except in the wintertime, when the canals were dandy for skating.

The Pilgrims, according to William Bradford, "...saw many goodly and fortified cities, strongly walled and guarded...Also they heard a strange and uncouth language, and beheld the different manners and customs of the people, with their strange fashions."

Like many an immigrant before and since, the Scrooby congregation had to climb three big mountains: learn the language, find homes, get jobs. And it wasn't as if Holland was such a peaceful place then. Dutchmen, with the help of Myles Standish and other English soldiers, were fighting against the cruel control of Spain. Except for the truce-time between 1609 and 1621, the struggle went on for almost a hundred years, from the mid-1500s until Dutch independence in 1648. So the Dutch were sympathetic to the Jews from Portugal, Protestants from England, and plenty of other desperate people who were fleeing from bad-behaving governments. Because these refugees brought their skills and talents with them, Holland became, despite its Spanish troubles, rich and powerful.

1597

Storms scatter a second Spanish Armada. Still, Spain's empire is at its height. The lands and peoples of Mexico, Central America, some of South America, much of the West Indies, and what will be the southwestern United States are under the shadow of the Spanish Crown.

In Iceland, volcano Mount Hekla erupts.

After about a year, thanks to some mighty hot arguments over religious teachings, the Separatists' congregation splits apart. Williams Bradford and Brewster went with the breakaway flock, away from Amsterdam. About a hundred members of "the Christian Reformed religion" got permission to move to the small, "fair and beautiful city" of Leyden (nowadays spelled Leiden). There they'd stay for the next 11 years, until 1620.

THE FAIR AND BEAUTIFUL CITY

✳

LEYDEN WAS FAMOUS FOR SURVIVING the horrid, deadly time back in 1574 when Spanish soldiers surrounded the city walls for months, starving the brave, stubborn people inside. Outside, the Dutch cut the dikes, sailing to the rescue on the flooding-in sea. Now, in 1609, Leyden was known for its canals lined with linden trees, its cloth-making industry, and its great university.

1598

With death of **Fyodor I, Boris Godunov** becomes the official Czar of Russia.

September 13 – **Philip II** is dead. Long live **Philip III**, King of Spain.

September 18 – **Toyotomi Hideyoshi**, Japanese dictator, dies. Warlord **Tokugawa Ieyasu** is gathering power.

What did William Bradford, his friends, and even their little kids do there? Worked hard, long hours for very little money. They combed wool or made such things as hats, gloves, buttons, chairs, ribbons, or beer, which even children and the godly drank rather than get sick from available drinking water. William eventually became a weaver. He made a sturdy cloth called fustian. Their pastor, Reverend John Robinson (Reverend Clyfton stayed in Amsterdam), studied and taught in the university along with Protestant students from all over Europe. Latin was the common language of all scholars, but some German and Danish students wanted to learn English, too. William Brewster gave them lessons.

Where did they live? Mostly in the narrow lanes near the University and the old *Pieterskerk* (St. Peter's Church). William probably lived with the Brewsters in *Stincksteeg* (Stink Alley). Later on, having sold a bit of English land he'd inherited, 23-year-old William, newly made citizen of Leyden, bought a little house for himself and his 16-year-old bride, Dorothy May from Amsterdam.

The church members scraped up money for a house called *Groenepoort* (Green Gate), where their well-loved pastor

---

1598

Juan de Oñate *leads a wagon train with 400 men, women, and children. They and 7,000 head of livestock set off north across the Rio Grande to colonize Pueblo territory (modern-day New Mexico). The fierce desert there became known as La Journada del Muerto (Journey of the Dead Man).*

1599

A fine pair of future painters and one future soldier/statesman are born: **Anthony Van Dyck, Diego Velazquez,** *and* **Oliver Cromwell.**

and his family could live and the fellowship could worship. A happy bonus: There was enough land around Green Gate for the congregation's carpenters to build 21 little houses for the members.

How did they worship? Early Sunday mornings, they gathered and prayed (standing, not kneeling as folks did in the Churches of England and Rome), and sang (no fancy organ, just voices). Black-clad, black-gloved Pastor Robinson or Ruling Elder Brewster read verses from the Geneva Bible, which had been translated by Calvinist scholars in the 1550s over in Switzerland. (You may be sure that their congregation had no use for King James's authorized version of the Scriptures, published in 1611.) Then they listened to fine preaching (several hours' worth), took a dinner break, and came back for general discussion (men talking, women listening) in the afternoon.

So they lived in the fair and beautiful city of Leyden. "Being thus settled (after many difficulties)," William wrote later on, "they continued many years in a comfortable condition, enjoying much sweet delightful society and spiritual comfort together in the ways of God."

1600

There are about 550 million earthlings in 1600, one of them being teenage Myles Standish. The slave trade is affecting African kingdoms such as the Bakongo; nearly 900,000 are working in the New World. Protestant and Catholic Europeans fight each other and worry about the mighty Muslim Ottoman Empire. Russia is expanding, and in India, the Mogul Empire glitters with art and learning. Spanish, English, and Portuguese traders are competing hard against the Dutch, who'll have more ships at sea than all the rest by the time the 1600s come to an end.

WHY?

*

SO WHY WOULD THEY EVER LEAVE LEYDEN? After all that they had been through, why would they want to go so far away?

For one thing, maybe William Bradford meant that they were "comfortable" compared to their sufferings before they got to Leyden and after they left. They did their best to be cheerful, but truly, life was tough. It was hard, working and living in a foreign land, so hard that some of the folks went back. They'd rather risk an English jail than be free in a land which could never be home.

For another, they were afraid for their children, surrounded by foreign language, ideas, and prosperous Hollanders who saw Sunday as a day for sleigh-riding, feasting, and other pleasures. Their kids were in danger of melting into a Dutch pot, losing their English ways, and straying from their parents' idea of a

1600

Eurydice, *the first grand opera, is sung in Florence, Italy.*

In London, in his newly built Globe Theater, **Richard Burbage** *performs Hamlet, in* **William Shakespeare's** *newest play.*

William Gilbert, *an English physician, publishes "De Magnete," introducing the world to such terms as "electric force" and "magnetic pole."*

godly life. Already, as Bradford recorded, some of the younger generation had become soldiers, gone to sea, or other "extravagant and dangerous courses."

And the drums of war were beating. Off in Germany and Bohemia, Protestants and Catholics were fighting. Churches smashed up. Folks tossed out of windows broke their necks on the bloody cobblestones down below. Who knew that the fighting would spread, last 30 years, and kill more than 8 million people? No one. But the Pilgrims, poor foreigners with unpopular beliefs, figured that war could only make their situation more uncertain.

They knew that the temporary peace between Holland and Spain would be ending in 1621. That was bad enough, but now, in 1619, the Pilgrims faced a more immediate crisis. Their old enemy, the king of England, had never declared a truce in his fight against folks who went against him and his Church. King James I was on the warpath against "a certain Brownist of Leyden," none other than Elder William Brewster, who'd gone into the printing business. Shortly after James got hold of one of the books he'd printed, Brewster had fled into hiding.

The Rozwi people of southern Africa build up Zimbabwe, the great city of the Changamire Empire.

In Prague, **Tycho Brahe**, *court astronomer to* **Rudolf II**, *head of the Holy Roman Empire (it was a part of Europe ruled by German kings ever since the year 962), begins working with younger math whiz and skywatcher* **Johannes Kepler**.

Thanks to helpful church and university friends who bravely pointed the king's men in wrong directions, Brewster led his pursuers on a merrie olde wild goose chase on both sides of the North Sea. And if he'd gotten caught? A minister from Scotland who'd printed a similar book was sentenced to pay a fine of 3,000 pounds (about $150,000). Then, before his life imprisonment began, he was to be whipped, have his head and hands locked into a wooden pillory so the public could see him get his ears cut off, his nose slit, and his face branded with the letters "S.S." for Stirrer of *Sedition* (making people rise up against their government).

In the time of the Pilgrims, independent thought was a matter of life and death. Brave as they were, they were fearful of staying and fearful of going. Still, more of the members of the little church voted to remain in Holland than risk crossing the ocean to face heaven-only-knew what horrifying dangers. But for the Pilgrims, working hard for land of their very own, where they could think, write, speak, and worship as they saw fit without being chased away: Those were temptations which they could not deny. They knew it would be tough, but, as William Bradford would write, "all great and honorable actions are

1601

Death of **Tycho Brahe**, astronomer.

Explorer **Juan de Oñate** searches Kansas — in vain — for the fabled Quivira, the golden kingdom.

Soldier **John Smith** of future Jamestown fame is fighting Turks in Europe when he's captured and sold into slavery (see 1603).

accompanied with great difficulties and must be both enterprised and overcome with answerable courages. It was granted the dangers were great, but not desperate."

It would be rotten, but not impossible.

WHERE WOULD THEY GO?

✳

AS EARLY AS 1617, MEN OF THE FELLOWSHIP — John Carver, Robert Cushman, and William Brewster — went to England to look into the possibility of going to America. They had to find *adventure capitalists* (men to put up money for an expedition) and get a *patent* (official, detailed permissions to set up a colony). Doing those things was much easier said than done. Meanwhile, the congregation debated about where in the New World they would make their stand.

They considered land near the Kennebec River, in present-day

1602

English sailor **Will Adams** takes a Japanese name: **Anshin Miura.** He survives a shipwreck near the coast of Japan where he remains for the rest of his life, building boats.

The Dutch East India Company is formed. Its aim: trade in precious pepper, ginger, cinnamon, and such grown in the Spice Islands of Indonesia.

English mariner **Bartholomew Gosnold** sails around Cape Cod.

Maine, where English colonists had failed to establish a colony in 1607~08 because it was too, too cold. Some of the fellowship very much wanted the "perpetual spring" described in Sir Walter Ralegh's book about Guiana, but a majority of the members decided northeastern South America was too close to Spanish territory. Sir Walter himself might have told them that. Disobeying King James's orders, he went into Spain's South American lands to hunt for El Dorado, the mythical city of gold. Having found only Spanish soldiers, he returned to England and got his head chopped off in 1618.

What about Virginia? It had been 11 years since Englishmen had established the Jamestown settlement. It is likely that the Pilgrims knew of the recent death, in 1617, in England of Mrs. John Rolfe, a.k.a. Pocahontas, "Indian princess." They certainly knew that nine out of ten colonists had died over there, from starvation, disease, and dreadful attacks by their native-born neighbors, who'd been treated rather badly by the famous Captain John Smith.

While the Pilgrims were in Leyden, Captain Smith was exploring the land around and beyond Massachusetts Bay, a region he called New England. Going there was not the

1602

Turkish and Persian soldiers march off to fight each other.

1603

African warrior-diplomat **King Idris Alooma** *dies after 32 years on the throne of Kanem-Borno.*

Black Death *returns to kill thousands of English folks. Famine stalks Russia. Tens of thousands die of hunger.*

Captain Smith and his fellow adventurers catch sight of the New World.

Pilgrims' game plan. They hoped to end up farther south, at the mouth of the river named after explorer Henry Hudson. If they had, they'd have come to the future site of New York City, a little ways south of 41° latitude, the northern boundary of Virginia territory. It would have been five years before Dutchmen would pay 60 guilders (about $24) to some Algonquian folks for Manhattan Island. Here is not the place for imagining how history would have been different if the

1603

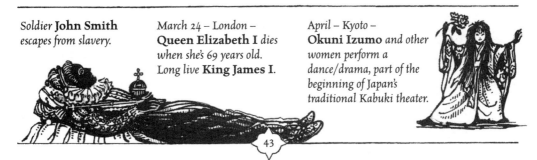

Soldier **John Smith** escapes from slavery.

March 24 – London – **Queen Elizabeth I** *dies when she's 69 years old.* Long live **King James I**.

April – Kyoto – **Okuni Izumo** *and other women perform a dance/drama, part of the beginning of Japan's traditional Kabuki theater.*

Pilgrims had gotten there first. They would, in fact, arrive at the edge of Massachusetts in 1620, but only after a long muddle and more than one near disaster.

In Leyden, Pastor Robinson and other leaders of his congregation met Thomas Weston, a bold, big-promising, fast-talking businessman who represented about 70 other Merchant Adventurers. These investors were in the business of backing folks willing to sell all they had and risk their lives to take on wild America. In many a letter between London and Leyden, the would-be colonists and the moneymen argued over the details of their business agreement. They'd have seven years to repay their investors by working every day, farming, fishing, trapping, and wood-chopping. They would have to build homes and barns in their spare time. And of course, they could only do all of this if, by the grace of God, they survived the ocean crossing and were not killed by their native neighbors who might not care for newcomers infesting the landscape.

It was a tough deal, but still, in the spring of 1620, the Pilgrims hired a sea captain and crew and bought a small, two-masted ship called *Speedwell*, a crummy name, considering how things would turn out.

1603

Edo (present-day Tokyo) – **Tokugawa Ieyasu** *is the new shogun (leader). His ancestors will rule until 1867. During most of this time, the Japanese will become more isolated.*

1604

October 11 – Prague – **Johannes Kepler** *observes a new star, a supernova. It means, he believes, that* **Aristotle** *of ancient Greece was wrong: The heavens can change.*

WHO WOULD GO? WHO WOULD STAY?

✳

THERE WAS NEVER ENOUGH MONEY for all of them to go to sea. Since most of "ye Saints" were staying put in Holland, Pastor Robinson would be with them, hoping to bring more of his flock over the waves as soon as they could. By the way, William Bradford didn't mean "Saints" the way Roman Catholics use the term — that he and his friends were officially, especially holy. He meant that they were members of God's church. His old friend, William Brewster (hiding somewhere in England), would be their pastor in America – if he could avoid getting arrested.

They'd pretty much decided that only the youngest and strongest would attempt the daring voyage. Some of the Pilgrims, fearing the dangerous voyage and knowing that the first year in America would be the hardest, made what must have been heartbreaking choices to split up their families. That way,

1605

John Hawkins *brought tobacco from America in 1565. Now, many a pipe is smoked in England but not by* King James I! *He writes that the custom is "loathsome to the eye, hateful to the nose, harmful to the brain...."*

April 13 – Moscow –
Czar Boris Godunov, *52, dies. His son* **Fyodor** *takes over and is soon murdered. A man who says he's the long-lost son of* **Ivan IV** *grabs the throne! This "false Dimitri" rules Russia for almost a year (see 1591).*

those who were too young, such as William Bradford's only child, or too old or puny could avoid the worst hardships and come later, when the colony was established. And that way, at least some of the family would survive if their dear ones died in the ocean or in the harsh New World. Cold comfort for William's young wife, Dorothy, having to leave their five-year-old John in Holland. Wasn't William and Susannah White's boy the same age? Wasn't he coming? Yes, but each head of household did what he thought best: William's wife and child (Dorothy and little John) must obey.

Folks quit jobs, sold houses and furniture, and gave themselves no choice but to go. Their bridges were burned. But with passing time, second thoughts, disagreements over destinations, and other things made more than one would-be-traveler change his mind and ask for his money back. What a lot of this boiled down to was that the possible colony needed more colonists.

The investors took matters into their own hands. They rustled up a bunch of folks over in England, including a few they'd hired, such as a young cooper, John Alden, to look after the ship's kegs and barrels, and a tough army veteran, Myles Standish, to be the colony's military adviser. Unlike the Leyden

1605

October 17 — India —
Akbar, 62, long known for his wisdom and toleration of non-Muslims, dies. He'd reigned over the Mogul Empire for 49 years.

Guy Fawkes

November 5 —
On this day **Guy Fawkes** meant to blow up the king and the Parliament because of their harsh anti-Catholic laws. He was nabbed before his "Gunpowder Plot" could succeed. Guy Fawkes Day is still an English holiday.

folks, these other travelers weren't necessarily looking for religious freedom. Maybe they wanted land or adventure or a chance to reinvent themselves in the New World. Some were servants without much say in the matter. In any case, they were called Strangers because, generally, the Saints didn't know them.

Robert Cushman, of the Leyden congregation, and Thomas Weston, the moneymen's man, did something else, too: They hired the services of Christopher Jones, master and part-owner of the *Mayflower*. He and his crew would bring the Strangers, including Captain Myles Standish and his wife, from London. They'd all be waiting at Southampton, England, for the *Speedwell* and the Saints.

Miguel de Cervantes, *former soldier, pirate-captive, and slave, publishes Part I of one of the earliest novels:* Don Quixote de la Mancha (*see 1615 for Part II*).

William Shakespeare *writes* King Lear *and* Macbeth.

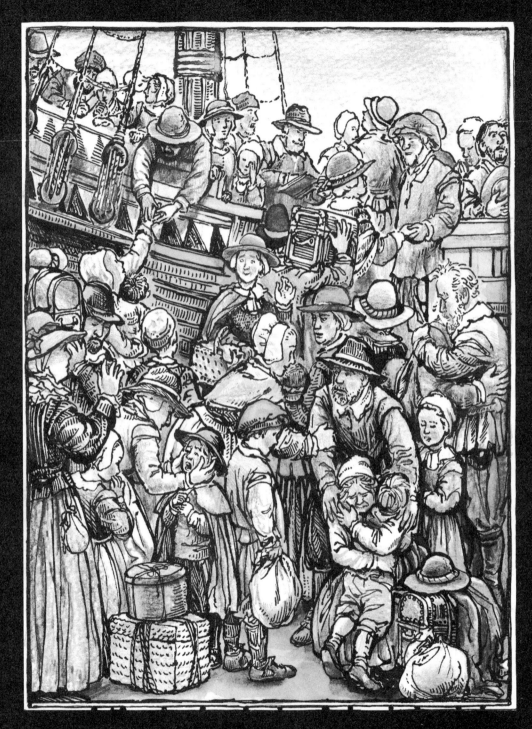

Sad good-byes at Delfthaven

CHAPTER THREE

So Long, Old World

FAREWELLS

*

AFTER NEARLY THREE YEARS OF DEBATING, praying, and preparing, it was time to leave. Most of the congregation piled into canal boats and went along with the travelers to see them off. They left the "goodly and pleasant city," their home for nearly 12 years, but, Bradford would write, "they knew they were pilgrims and looked not much on those things but lifted their eyes to the heavens, their dearest country, and quieted their spirits." The boats glided along, past ancient trees, a little over 20 miles to Delfthaven. Then, one summer day in 1620, "with mutual embraces and many tears they took their leaves

1605	1606	
La Villa Real de la Santa Fe de San Francisco de Asis, otherwise known as Santa Fe, in present-day New Mexico, is founded. 	July 15 – **Rembrandt van Rijn,** future painter, is born in Leyden, Holland.	English navigator **Martin Pring** explores the coasts of Maine and Massachusetts.

one of another." Many a dear one, such as Dorothy Bradford and little John, never saw each other ever again, not on this earth anyway.

After all of the sad good-byes and a damp journey on the North Sea and into the English Channel in the not too shipshape *Speedwell*, there were plenty of greetings as the Leyden travelers met Myles and Rose and the other Strangers aboard the *Mayflower*. There was at least one happy hello when a mysterious "Mr. Williamson" came out of hiding below decks. The Saints

---

THE CALENDAR GETS AN UPDATE

*F*or more accurate timekeeping, Pope Gregory XIII and his astronomers changed the old *Julian* calendar, which Europeans had used since the time of Roman emperor Julius Caesar. How did they change it? By removing ten days from October 1582, only about two years before Myles Standish was born. But this new *Gregorian* calendar would not be accepted and used in the British Empire, which included its American colonies, of course, until 1752. When that happened, all of the old dates were moved up ten days. According to the old style Julian calendar, the Pilgrims left Holland on July 22, 1620. By the Gregorian calendar, which we still use today, the date was August 1, 1620. It was a sad day by any reckoning.

1606

Though **Luis Vaez de Torres** *sailed nearby, the first known European to land in Australia was Dutch mariner* **Willem Jansz.**

December 20 –
More than a hundred men, including captains **Christopher Newport, Bartholomew Gosnold,** *and* **John Smith,** *sail for Virginia on the* Godspeed, *the* Discovery, *and the* Susan Constant.

knew him, of course, as their beloved outlaw, William Brewster.

So they all sailed off to America, right? Not all of them. Not right away. And not without a boatload of trouble. First, a hot argument with Thomas Weston: The Pilgrims could not, would not sign a new, harsher agreement with the moneymen. It would have them working nearly every waking moment, logging, trapping, and trading to pay back the investors, with precious little time for building their own homes. Weston stomped away, mad. Second, the would-be colonists had to get the leaky *Speedwell* fixed. To pay the bill, they sold about two tons of the butter they'd packed. Then they had to turn around twice, to the seaports of Dartmouth, then two weeks in Plymouth, England, for more repairs because the *Speedwell* still leaked!

Horrible seasickness! Terrible delays! The Leyden Saints had to give up on the *Speedwell* along with their hopes of having their own ship in America. Bad luck — or worse. William Bradford thought the *Speedwell's* cunning Captain Reynolds made his ship unseaworthy on purpose to get out of going on the hard journey. Any sort of dark deed-doer could be hired in a rough seaport town like Plymouth, England, home base for many an English pirate. Only with a time machine and a lot of

1607

May 14 –
Christopher Newport *of the London Company founds a settlement to be known as Jamestown, in honor of the king of England.* **Captain John Smith** *will be in charge of the colony.*

"Flight of the Earls." Irish noblemen, afraid of being arrested for rising up against the English, flee. They wind up finding sanctuary in Rome.

sneaky peeking and listening could we ever know this for sure, or, for that matter, the other 40 gazillion things we'd love to know about the past.

In any event, though the *Mayflower* was at least twice as big as the *Speedwell*, everything and everyone could never fit into one ship. Twenty people would have to stay behind and, given all that'd happened, it probably wasn't hard to get volunteers. Still, in spite of their troubles, there was another man in Plymouth who wanted to come with the Pilgrims. But they declined the services of the famous Captain John Smith, explorer of Massachusetts Bay. After all, they weren't going there. Anyway, it was cheaper to buy his book, A *Description of New England*, than pay for the author. The grizzled veteran of Jamestown might well have been shaking his head at the idea of these brave amateurs — these ragged men, women, and children — taking on the wilderness.

Did Myles and Rose Standish squeeze each other's hands as the *Mayflower* sailed into the English Channel? As the buildings of Plymouth got smaller and smaller? Did they shade their eyes and squint up at Master Jones? There he stood, up on the lofty poop deck, taking them sailing into the west and away, September 6, 1620.

1607

December –
At least 50 Jamestown colonists are dead of hunger and illness. **Captain John Smith**, off searching for food, is captured by native warriors. According to the captain, he might have been killed – if 12-year-old **Pocahontas** had not begged her father to spare his life.

1608

July 7 – Canada –
Samuel de Champlain begins a settlement. It is called Québec.

HOW MASTER JONES NAVIGATED

$\mathcal{W}$hen all around him was sky and water, how in the world did a sea captain know where his ship was? For one thing, he'd have a compass. It may be that Chinese and Mediterranean sailors had been using them since the year 1000. With his cross-staff, he'd check the positions of the sun and stars as compared to the horizon. Once he checked his charts and his book of numerical tables, and did some clever calculating, Master Jones would have a fair idea of the *Mayflower's* latitude. Almost 150 years would pass before clockmaker John Harrison would devise a way for sailors to calculate longitude.

So he could track where his ship was on his map and figure out when and where he'd make landfall, Master Jones needed to know something else. For a speedometer he used a chip log, a piece of wood to which a long, evenly knotted rope had been attached. As the chip floated, as he counted the knots passing through his hands, as he kept track of the time, he would know how fast his ship was sailing.

1608

Galileo *builds his first compound-lens optic glass, a.k.a. the telescope. It was invented earlier this year by Dutch lens maker* **Hans Lippershey.**

1609

Spain and Holland agree to a truce: they'll quit fighting for a dozen years.

WHAT DID THEY BRING?

*B*esides their boxes and trunks, the travelers were going to need chairs, tables, benches, stools, beds, cradles, chests, and cupboards full of bedding, tablecloths, and napkins. Mattresses were coarse cloth bags stuffed with straw. (As for their clothes, see page 109.)

There would be looms and spinning wheels as well as pots, kettles, and pans; candlesticks, crocks, pewter plates, mugs, knives, spoons, and *trenchers* (wooden plates); buckets, baskets, hourglasses and sundials; mortars and pestles for grinding precious spices, such as nutmeg, cinnamon, and pepper.

They had to bring plenty of food that would keep. It had to last them a long time. The voyage could last two months or more, and they could expect no grocery stores in wild America. Sacks of onions, beans, cabbages, peas, turnips, and parsnips, as well as barrels of salted or smoked or pickled or dried beef, pork, or codfish. Boxes of smoked herring, hardtack, cheese, and dried ox tongues. Tubs of pickled eggs. Barrels of oatmeal and flour.

Casks of butter and beer. Salt. Sugar, molasses, raisins, and prunes. Holland gin. French brandy. Pipes and tobacco.

They packed a bewildering collection of tools including axes, hatchets, hammers, chisels, hoes, spades, sickles, saws, shovels, scythes, rakes, mattocks for digging, hayforks, *holdfasts* (vises), plus hooks, nets, nails, rope, twine, and grain and seed for field crops and gardens.

Military advisor Myles would have made certain that the colonists packed muskets, powder, flints, shot, cannon balls, swords, daggers, cutlasses, their armor, of course, plus a drum and a trumpet for military parades and special occasions. Four cannon, a couple of big guns (each weighing 1,200 pounds) and two more, even bigger guns completed their arsenal.

For trading with the Indians, they packed beads, knives, rings, bracelets, mirrors, and cloth. For reading and teaching, they brought Bibles, books, almanacs, and *hornbooks* (ABCs, etc. pasted on a board, protected with clear horn). Myles Standish brought several books, including a world history and *Julius Caesar's Commentaries*, about the warrior-emperor's battles in *Gaul* (ancient France). [Read more about Myles's books on page 129.]

For nearly 15 years, the *Mayflower* had hauled barrels of tar, herring, boxes of hats, bolts of cloth, and casks of French wine from one European port to another. Because wine smelled good, the *Mayflower* was called a "sweet ship," a reputation lost long before her two-legged and four-legged passengers were done with her, what with wooden buckets serving as the ship's only bathrooms. It must have been awfully stinky!

It's likely that even tough, 36-year-old Myles Standish was seasick as a "fine small gale" blew the tiny ship out on the North Atlantic. Almost all of the other passengers were. These homesick, seasick, psalm-singing landlubbers got on the crew's nerves and got in their way as sailors worked the sails and the multitude of ropes that drove the ship. Little kids chattered or cried when men were trying to sleep. The crew cussed at and made fun of these "glib-gabbety puke-stockings," who began their days praying and singing on the upper deck. One in particular kept threatening to toss them all overboard -- until he got sick, so sick that he died. It was his body that went into the sea. Had God Himself, the superstitious sailors wondered, punished their big-mouthed buddy? They cut out the teasing, just in case.

1609

While exploring in the wilds to be known as Vermont, **Samuel de Champlain** *sees the big cold lake that will be named after him.*

In what will be New York, **Henry Hudson** *becomes the first European to explore the great river that will have his name.*

As folks got used to the ship's motion, they were able to keep their food in their stomachs. What kind of food? Pretty grim and mostly eaten cold because all there was to cook on was a little, sand-filled "hearth-box." They'd crumble crackers or *hardtack* (flat, hard biscuit) into their soups and stews. There'd be oatmeal, sweetened, perhaps, with molasses, and, for a favorite treat, plum duff, a raisin or prune-and-*suet* (beef fat) pudding. And to drink? Beer. Even little kids drank it. It had just enough alcohol, one percent or less, to kill the bacteria that might infest water. As a rule, people living in the colonial world had to be awfully thirsty and pretty desperate before they'd take a swig of water.

As the men got their sea legs, Myles Standish began drilling them in military ways so they could hunt and protect themselves in the wild New World. His face probably turned red and angry more than once, trying to teach former tailors, weavers, and what-not how to use big, heavy, matchlock muskets. Once they rammed gunpowder plus a ball plus a wad of paper into the barrel, they lit a *match* (a wick) which, when the trigger was pulled and the *serpentine* (hammer) came down, touched off a powder-filled flashpan. Then, if the match didn't go out and all went well, BOOM went the gun in a crashing cloud of smoke and with an

1610

Jesuit missionaries set up their first mission in Paraguay, hoping to convert the native Guaranî people to Roman Catholicism.

With his new telescope, **Galileo** discovers 4 of Jupiter's 16 moons.

almighty kick. A fellow could get his shoulder knocked out of joint or he could find himself flat on the deck on his behind.

CLENCHED FISTS DOWN IN THE DARK

*

MEANWHILE, IN THE DIM, SMELLY WORLD below deck, Rose Standish and the other women and girls tried to keep themselves and their families fed, reasonably warm, and tidy — hard enough when the sea was calm. What about when the wind turned cold and fierce, which it was bound to do so late in the season? What about when it howled, sending sailors scrambling high into the rigging to haul up the heavy sails and lash them tight? What about when gray-green, white-capped mountains of water thundered over the little ship? Master Jones ordered all passengers below, where it was nice and dry, right? Oh, no. Icy water streamed through opened-up cracks in the deck, onto freezing,

1610

Men aboard the Discovery sail through Hudson Strait and into Hudson Bay, both named after their captain, **Henry Hudson**.

Thanks to Indians slaving in the silver and gold mines, Spaniards are getting rich in the boom town of Potosí in present-day Bolivia.

screaming kids and terrified grownups, while Elder Brewster urged them to have faith. Imagine the nights in that crowded, creaking blackness, wondering if the next wave will dash you to the bottom of the ocean!

Then, in the worst of the waves, a wooden beam cracked! Water poured in through the splintered deck as the *Mayflower* pitched and rolled. Was she falling apart? The colonists had brought along a big iron screw, sort of a giant tire jack, for raising heavy roof timbers. With it, the strongest men repaired the beam, but would it hold? Should they turn back to England? Or try to make for the coast of Africa? No, Master Jones wasn't ready to give up. He trusted his old ship. They'd go on.

But the storm didn't want to give up either. As it pounded on, one of the passengers got swept into the sea, a lot of which he swallowed before amazingly lucky John Howland grabbed a rope and got hauled aboard. It was into this hard, scary, miserable little world, in Master Jones's cabin at the stern of the ship, that a baby boy was born to Stephen Hopkins's wife, Elizabeth. They named him Oceanus. The *Mayflower* had one more passenger — then one less.

William Butten got very sick. On November 6, when they were almost to America, he died. It might well have been scurvy

1610

Deaths of three warrior/rulers and one popular artist: **Queen Amina** *in today's Nigeria, French* **King Henry IV** *(he's stabbed),* **King Ralambo** *of Madagascar's Merina kingdom, and* **Michelangelo Merisi da Caravaggio.**

that killed him. For thousands of years, this sickness had killed legions of sea-going folks who lived for months on rum, hardtack, and jerky. Not much, if any, vitamin C in those. Not until 1753, more than a 130 years in the future, would Dr. Lind of Scotland recommend that lemons and limes be added to sailors' diets.

ALMOST THERE

✳

MASTER JONES CONSIDERED HIS COMPASS and charts, the birds, the color of the water, even the smell of the air. Land was near! He ordered his men to drop a heavy line and try to find the ocean floor. Eighty fathoms! Hard earth lay a mere 480 feet below the glimmering surface of the sea. The bottom of the Atlantic was generally about 14,000 feet down, more (sea canyons twice that deep or deeper) or less (ridges half as deep or poking up as islands). Below the *Mayflower* was the shelflike edge of the New World.

1611

In James Bay, at the edge of Hudson Bay, the Discovery's starving men mutiny. They cast adrift **Henry Hudson**, his son, and a few loyal sailors. They're never seen again.

An English version of the Bible, its translation approved by His Majesty **King James I**, is published.

Since Plymouth, those poor, grubby, worn out wayfarers had spent more than two months in their cold, wet, prison. For those who had come from Holland, it was nearly twice that. Behind on that Thursday morning, November 9, 1620, was the rising sun and nearly three thousand miles of ocean. High above them was the lookout crying, "Land ahoy! L-a-a-a-nd HO!"

They'd made it.

Almost.

1612

In his *Map of Virginia,* **Captain John Smith** describes the land, its plants, creatures, and weather.

Jamestown, Virginia — **John Rolfe** *plants tobacco seeds he bought in the West Indies. Soon the dried, smokable leaves are a cash crop for the colony and for the English Crown.*

At last: America!

CHAPTER FOUR

April Showers Bring May Flowers

LAND HO!

*

DIRECTLY AHEAD OF THEM was the continent of North America—but where? Lo and behold, as the old storytellers used to say, they'd come to a peninsula extending out from New England! On maps it still looks like Massachusetts had stuck out its arm to show off its muscle.

This big arm had had many names. People probably had been living there at least 7,000 years. Viking explorers might have visited about the year 1000. John Cabot, a.k.a. Giovanni Caboto of Italy, might well have glimpsed this land when he sailed to America in 1498, under the flag of England. In 1525,

---

1612

In Ceylon (today's Sri Lanka), **Senarat**, the king of Kandy, makes a treaty with the Dutch, hoping for protection from the Portuguese.

1613

February 22 – Teenage **Czar Mikhail** (Michael) becomes Russia's first Romanov ruler. The dynasty will last until the revolution of 1917.

a Spanish explorer named the area Tierra de Esteban Gomez. Six years before the Pilgrims got there, Captain John Smith called the peninsula Cape James, in honor of the king, but it was another English explorer, Bartholomew Gosnold, back in 1602, who gave it the name that stuck: Cape Cod, in honor of the fish that he caught around there. This same Bartholomew was so impressed with the nearby island of Capawack and its grape vines that he gave it a new name: Martha's Vineyard, after his daughter.

In 1605, Samuel de Champlain, the great mapmaker and explorer, sailed around Cape Cod and New England, which was part of *New France* (the name for all the land claimed by France in North America) as far as this French adventurer was concerned. That same year, explorer George Weymouth visited thereabouts and decided to take a young Patuxet Indian with him back to England. Tisquantum learned English so well that he got a job as a translator for John Smith and a ride back home when the famous explorer came to Massachusetts in 1614. His adventures were only just beginning — but more about Tisquantum when we meet him later. By the way, you might know him better by his nickname: Squanto.

1613

Dutchmen set up a post on the tip of Manhattan Island, where they can trade for pelts and furs.

London – The **Globe Theater** goes up in flames.

1614

Pocahontas, *newly baptized into the Christian faith and having adopted the first name Rebecca, gets a new last name too,* and a husband: **John Rolfe.**

HARD ROCKS MEET ROUGH WATER

*

IN A PRETTY ELEGANT UNDERSTATEMENT, William Bradford wrote that he and his shipmates "were not a little joyful" to see land, but since they were aiming to settle farther south, they decided to keep sailing. Master Jones set his course down along the long arm of the Cape, heading for the mouth of Hudson's River. They might have made it if they hadn't been sailing during the stormiest time of the year and if they hadn't been going through some of the most dangerous, deadly waters on Earth!

They got as far south as Monomoy Point, a spit of land down at the big arm's elbow, also known as Cape Malabar. There, the Atlantic churned white and pounded hard against her rocky shore. Luck, fate, wind, grace, skills of the skipper and his crew, prayers of his passengers — choose all or any you like, but the *Mayflower* was saved from being ripped open and smashed to pieces.

Sir Walter Ralegh, *out of favor and locked up in the Tower of London, writes his History of the World.*

In Flanders *(present-day Belgium)*, **Peter Paul Rubens**, *one of the great artists of the 1600s, is making huge, brilliant paintings.*

They had to turn back. Not to England, just back up north to the Cape's upraised fist. The passengers were absolutely relieved to still be alive. On the other hand, they faced a very real problem.

John Carver, of the Leyden congregation, had proper papers giving them permission to begin a colony, but not up here. Back in Plymouth, England, the Saints had met with Sir Ferdinando Gorges who was sure he could get them a patent to settle in New England, but he wasn't quick enough. Now, here they were. You can bet that they were sick and tired of the ship, and right here before them was blessedly solid land, far away from the king's sheriffs and bishops. Maybe it was meant to be. And maybe, as far as some of the Strangers were concerned, this meant something else. If there wasn't specific legal authority to be here, then they didn't have to go by any rules handed out by these Holland Saints or those moneymen back in England, right?

Wrong. The men who'd been working on this enterprise for the last three years weren't about to let their colony fall apart before it even got started. They had to work this out *before* they landed. If not, anything might happen; a mutiny could lead to bloodshed!

1615

Galileo *is ordered to Rome. The Catholic Church is very mad at him for saying that the Earth orbits the Sun when everybody has always known that it's the other way around.*

The Dutch fight the Portuguese for control of the Moluccas (the Spice Islands) and win.

Miguel de Cervantes *writes* Don Quixote Part II.

All day Friday, November 10, Master Jones sailed 50 miles north along Cape Cod while below deck, his miserable, chilly passengers argued over the problem. It's easy to imagine sailors grumbling, women rolling their eyes, baby Oceanus Hopkins crying, and red-headed Myles Standish ready to bust.

THE MAYFLOWER COMPACT

✳

WHEN FOLKS JOINED THE CHURCH AT LEYDEN, they had entered into a covenant: a solemn promise to stick together. The Pilgrims knew that their colony needed some such hammered-out agreement to bind them, to serve as their common law — their legal authority — until they got a proper patent from the royal government. (This would not happen until the following summer.)

Perhaps William Brewster, who'd studied at the University of Cambridge, did much of the writing. Londoner Stephen

1615

Europeans are curious about the latest new New World thing: rubber from the jungles where native South Americans make instant shoes by dipping their feet in latex (milky juice from the rubber tree) and letting it dry.

Samuel de Champlain *discovers another great lake. It'll be called Huron, after the people who live thereabouts.*

LAKE HURON

Hopkins might have worked on it, too. He was educated, and he'd been to the New World before. In fact, he might have been part of a mutinous adventure in 1609, when a hurricane blew Virginia-bound ships on to Bermuda. It was news of this island adventure that might have been the inspiration for one of William Shakespeare's plays, *The Tempest*.

In any case, when the passengers awoke on Saturday morning, November 11, 1620, they gathered to consider the completed document, which to later generations became known as the Mayflower Compact.

Myles Standish and 40 other men (women, like children, had no civil rights) signed the Compact. In doing so, they agreed to be ruled by law. Not only did this quiet down the protesters — mostly — it showed, in a time of all-powerful monarchs, people's determination to govern themselves. And another thing: The man they chose as the colony's governor was decidedly not Elder Brewster. Church and state would be separate, thank you very much. They elected John Carver.

Folks crowded the decks, feasting their hungry eyes on the sight of trees: oaks, birches, pines, and junipers, growing clear down to the water's edge. They saw sandy dunes, too, reminding

1616

London –
Mrs. John Rolfe, *a.k.a.* "*Indian princess*" **Pocahontas,** *and His Majesty* **King James I** *meet each other.*

April 23 –
Two of the best writers ever die on the same day: **William Shakespeare,** *in London;* **Miguel de Cervantes,** *in Madrid.*

THE MAYFLOWER COMPACT

*I*N THE NAME OF GOD, AMEN. *We whose names are underwritten, the loyal subjects of our dread Sovereign Lord, King James, by the Grace of God of Great Britain, France, Ireland, King, Defender of the Faith, etc.*

Having undertaken, for the Glory of God and advancement of the Christian Faith and Honour of our King and Country, a voyage to plant the First Colony in the Northern Parts of Virginia, do by these presents solemnly and mutually in the presence of God and one of another, covenant and combine ourselves together into a Civil Body Politic, for our better ordering and preservation and furtherance of the ends aforesaid, and by virtue hereof to enact, constitute and frame such just and equal laws, ordinances, Acts, Constitutions and Offices from time to time, as shall be thought most meet and convenient for the general good of the Colony, unto which we promise all due submission and obedience. In witness whereof we have hereunder subscribed our names at Cape Cod, the eleventh of November, in the year of the reign of our Sovereign Lord King James of England, France, and Ireland the eighteenth, and of Scotland the fifty-fourth. Anno Domini 1620.

some of Holland. For people used to long-settled countrysides, villages, and cities, it must have looked awfully desolate.

Think what it must have been like. More than 3,000 miles of immense ocean lies between you and home. Everyone's cold,

1616

In the far north by Greenland, **William Baffin** discovers what will be named Baffin Bay.

In the far south, Dutch mariner **Willem Schouten** is the first European to sail in the very stormy waters around South America's southern tip, which he names Cape Horn.

damp, smelly, filthy, and tired after months of hard travel and now — no one to welcome you. No inns. Not even a town to go to. And what if people suddenly appear and attack you? William Bradford started writing his history ten years after he and his friends got to New England, but he hadn't forgotten what it was like: "...a hideous and desolate wilderness, full of wild beasts and wild men....What could now sustain them but the Spirit of God and his grace?"

It's easy to imagine Myles Standish looking at Rose and asking himself what had he gotten them into?

THE FIRST YEAR 1620~1621

✳

MASTER JONES DROPPED ANCHOR a little ways out in what's nowadays called Provincetown Harbor. Men got to work unshipping the shallop, the small boat they'd brought along for short trips.

1616

Sea captain **Thomas Hunt** *kidnaps* **Tisquantum**, *a.k.a.* **Squanto**, *from Patuxet, takes him to Spain, and sells him into slavery. Some of Hunt's sailors leave germs behind — the beginning of a deadly epidemic (see 1618).*

1617

Sir Walter Ralegh *sets off for the Spanish Main. He sends an expedition up the Orinoco River (in present-day Venezuela) to look for gold. The men find nothing but angry Spaniards.*

Unfortunately, folks had been sleeping in it for the past months, and it'd need a lot of work before it could be trusted to float. Meanwhile, as the ship's crew put the *Mayflower* to rights, Myles Standish and 15 men put on their armor. Taking up their muskets and axes, they piled into the *Mayflower's* much larger longboat for a ride to shore. They'd go check things out to make sure it was safe for the other passengers to set foot on this foreign land.

The First Expedition · Saturday, November 11, 1620

* * *

Myles and the others kept their eyes peeled for Indians, what Europeans had called Native Americans ever since Columbus thought he'd finally made it to the *Indies* (India and the lands and islands of Southeast Asia) in 1492. Indian was a term born in ignorance, but it was nicer than "savage," "barbarian," and other names tossed around as one world invaded another.

The men cut a load of firewood before going back to the ship, but they found no fresh water, which a colony must have. They found no Indians either, not that day anyway, or the next: Sunday. Perhaps the ship's crew went fishing.

1618

Pocahontas, *a.k.a.* **Rebecca Rolfe**, *dies of smallpox when she's only 22 years old. She leaves behind her husband,* **John**, *and their baby son,* **Thomas**.

King Gustavus Adolphus *and* **Czar Mikhail** *sign a treaty: Swedish troops will leave Russia; Russia will give up access to the Baltic Sea.*

Sir Walter Ralegh *goes back to London where he's put to death for going into Spanish territory against the king's orders.*

Certainly they grumbled about these earnest psalm-singers who flatly refused to break their Sabbath by going ashore.

Monday now, that was another matter.

Imagine being cooped up for weeks and at last being able to walk on solid earth! Sun shining, gulls squawking, kids like four-year-old Mary Allerton and five-year-old Resolved White running and yelling. Maybe Mrs. Bradford watched, sad and silent, thinking about her own little boy back in Holland.

Imagine finding clams and mussels in the sand after weeks of horrid food, and don't think too much about the bellyaches later on. They found a pond, too: fine for washing piles of laundry. Soon stockings and linens were flapping off the old ship's rails and riggings. And imagine seeing whales swimming in Cape Cod Bay on such a day!

The Second Expedition · November 15~17

* * *

The colonists needed a place with fertile soil for planting, with fresh water and a fine, deep harbor where ships could come and go. They absolutely had to pick a good spot to settle and the sooner the better! Winter was bearing down hard. They were

1618

May 23 – Prague –
Catholics in Bohemia (today's Czech Republic) close a pair of Protestant churches. Protestants fight back by throwing a pair of Catholic leaders out of a palace window. This "defenestration" (derived from fenestra, the Latin word for "window") starts 30 years of miserable, destructive fighting all over Europe.

In Brussels (capital of modern-day Belgium), the world's very first pawnshop opens for business.

both nervous about Indians and eager to meet them. They hoped to — had to — trade with and learn from them. Myles Standish led William Bradford, Stephen Hopkins, and 13 others on another discovery mission. It wasn't long before they saw some people (they were likely of the Pamet tribe) and an Indian dog, too. They all took one look at red-bearded Myles, leading a file of helmeted musketeers, and vanished into the trees, even the dog! But the Englishmen wanted to talk! And, hey, what if there were more Indians hiding in the woods, waiting to ambush them, thinking they were scared? Myles led his troops on a chase!

Did they find their shy neighbors? No. They got lost. But they found a spring, and to these thirsty men, their first taste of New England water was "as pleasant to them as wine or beer." They found harvested fields and canoes and graves. They disturbed one, digging until they revealed a bow, arrows, and white bones. Myles and the men gazed on the long-dead warrior, then covered him over.

William Bradford got himself yanked UP and dangling from a tree, finding out the hard way how an Indian deer trap worked! Later, at a place still known as Corn Hill, they found

1619

Along America's east coast, thousands of natives, including neighbors and kinfolk of **Pocahontas** and **Squanto**, are dying of smallpox. At Jamestown, the Virginia House of Burgesses, the New World's first legislature, is called to order.

The first boatload of kidnapped Africans arrive in Virginia to begin the rest of their lives in slavery.

buried baskets of yellow, red, and blue ears. They took as much as they could — for seed — promising themselves to pay for it later, which they did. After three days and two nervous nights in the outdoors, Myles and the other men got back to the ship.

The Third Expedition · November 28~30

* * *

The men went farther south, this time with the shallop and the longboat. Master Jones and nine of his crew decided to come along. Myles and the other explorers found a pair of rounded huts. Inside were wooden bowls, clay pots, and intricate baskets, but where were the people? When they disturbed another grave, they found bowls, beads, and the bones of a man and a child. Still on the dead man's skull was his long blond hair: a mystery! Meanwhile, back on the *Mayflower*, most of the chilly, weary passengers huddled together, coughing and miserable. One, young Edward Thompson, died.

Some of the colonists wanted to plant their colony at Corn Hill, but, no, with so much at stake, there must be one more search. They couldn't afford a bad choice now. As Myles and the men were preparing for their mission, 14-year-old Francis

1619

A controversial book! **Johannes Kepler** *writes that planets' orbits are oval-shaped and not, as folks have believed for 2,000 years, circular.*

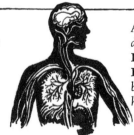

A ground-breaking discovery in London! **Dr. William Harvey** *shows how blood circulates in the human body.*

Billington began playing with a musket — right next to a barrel of gunpowder — and just about blew up the *Mayflower*. He probably didn't mean to.

Myles Standish, John Carver, William Bradford, John Howland, and the Tilley brothers (Edward and John), Stephen Hopkins, his servant (Edward Doty), Richard Warren, and the *Mayflower's* first and second mates (John Clarke and Robert Coppin), along with the ship's gunner and some sailors, set out on the fourth journey.

It was terrible.

The Fourth Expedition · December 6~11

* * *

In the evening of the first day, they saw, from a safe distance, maybe 10 or 12 men cutting up what looked like a small black whale, a "grampus" the sailors called it. At nightfall, the explorers built a fire and a "barricado," a small, three-sided shelter of branches and saplings. Myles would have taken his turn standing watch, probably squinting his eyes against the freezing wind, considering the Indians' faraway spark of a campfire off in the blackness.

The next day, the explorers divided up, one group in the shallop

1620

Sir Francis Bacon *of England publishes some of his writings about how to gather and judge evidence. His theories influence generations of scientists and other truth-seekers.*

In Kyoto, Japan, the Imperial Palace of Katsura is built.

Dutch Scientist **Cornelius Drebble** *builds the first workable submarine by covering a rowboat with animal hides.*

following the shore, the other tramping about, investigating. After a hard day full of icy wind and rain, a howling "hideous and great cry" pierced the night and yanked the exhausted men awake.

"Arm, arm!" cried the man on guard. The men managed to blast away with their muskets, great thundering flashes scaring off whomever might be sneaking around. Wolves, perhaps. Try and get some sleep. They did, until five in the morning when they were making breakfast. Again the horrifying cries. And arrows!

"Men, Indians! Indians!"

Myles Standish started shooting as others raced to get their guns, still others charging at the warriors with their cutlasses. The men fired up their blunderbusses and, Bradford remembered, "let fly." Myles took careful aim at one particular tree. Whoever was behind it had been shooting one arrow after another. In the next instant, bark and splinters exploded! The archer shrieked, and the attackers melted into the woods.

Some of the coats hanging on the shelter were full of arrows, but amazingly, their owners escaped unperforated. Leaving orders that the shallop be guarded, Myles marched about a dozen of the men into the forest, where they bellowed a defiant shout or two and blasted away with their guns. He wasn't

1620

1621

The Thirty Years' War rages on in Europe. Swedes and Turks are fighting the Poles; Protestants and Catholics are fighting each other.

A couple of firsts: London gets regular printed newsletters from the continent of Europe, and potatoes are planted in Germany.

Holland — Merchants begin the Dutch West India Company.

In the Low Countries, the Dutch and Spanish go back to fighting.

going to have anybody thinking that they were afraid! That would be deadly dangerous.

But they must have been scared — certainly they were miserable — when they nearly froze to death after wild water smashed their rudder AND their mast AND their sail fell overboard. The colonists piled into what was left of their boat and found Thievish Harbor. That's what Robert Coppin, the *Mayflower*'s second mate, called it anyway, in honor of the time he'd been there on an earlier voyage, when someone swiped a harpoon. The spot had had other names: Whitson Bay, Port du Cap St. Louis, Cranes Bay, Patuxet, Accomack. Captain John Smith had been there, too, back in 1614. He called it Plymouth. Whether or not preceded by "New," it's a place of many spellings: Plimouth, Plimoth, Plimmoth.

The little harbor wasn't deep enough to let the *Mayflower* — or any boat much bigger than the shallop — come any closer than a mile from shore, but beyond that shore, the men were delighted to find fresh water and cleared, tilled fields. The men tramped over land where corn had grown. Where were the people? Had something happened to them? And if they returned — what then? Still, Myles and his fellow explorers knew two things for sure:

1622

Marie de Gournay *of France writes a book,* On the Equality of Men and Women.

Jean Baptiste Poquelin, *a.k.a* **Moliere,** *is born in Paris. When he grows up, he'll be France's best-ever comic playwright.*

This was the best place they'd found, and everybody was desperate. They sailed back across the bay, eager to tell about what they'd discovered, not knowing that folks on the *Mayflower* were waiting with news of their own.

Mrs. White had given birth to a healthy boy and gave him a perfect name: Peregrine. It meant "pilgrim." With such happy news, why was everyone so sad? Why did they bow their heads when William Bradford climbed aboard the ship? Why did they avoid his eyes? Perhaps it fell to Elder Brewster, William's oldest friend, to tell him that 23-year-old Dorothy Bradford had fallen into the sea and drowned.

William Bradford, who noted the "little running brooks" at Plymouth and so much else, did not write about his wife's death. Was it because she might have gone overboard on purpose? If so, that would have been a dreadful sin. Or he may well have considered the subject too personal. Or he was too busy, too sad, and his heart was too full, especially when he thought about their little boy far away in Holland. Perhaps all of the above? Perhaps.

* * *

Not until December 18 — after Sunday was over — did the *Mayflower's* passengers start coming ashore. At Plymouth Rock?

1622   *1623*

Istanbul, Turkey – **Osman II**, the teenage sultan of the Ottoman Empire, is murdered.

OSMAN II

Madrid, Spain – **Diego Velasquez** *becomes the official painter at the court of* **King Philip IV**.

At Little Harbor, *Englishman* **David Thompson** *founds New Hampshire's first settlement at the site of the present-day town of Rye.*

Maybe. It was way off in 1741 when an old, old man, John Faunce, told folks that the Pilgrims had landed at that big, granite boulder in the harbor. People nowadays aren't *exactly* sure that the colonists first set foot there, but you can be sure the rock didn't have "1620" carved on it!

Back in 1620, the newcomers considered this or that spot. They argued. They prayed, and at last, on December 20, 1620, they chose a high hill overlooking the harbor for the center of their settlement. It would be known to those who lived there as New Plimoth Plantation.

As hard as their adventure had been, it was about to get even worse.

1624

Persians conquer Baghdad and all of Mesopotamia (present-day Iraq and a bit of Syria and Turkey).

In Japan, where Christians are persecuted more cruelly than ever, the shogun **Hidetada** dies. He'll be followed by his son **Iemitsu,** who'll kick all Spanish traders out of Japan.

King Louis XIII makes **Cardinal Richelieu,** already the most powerful man in France's government, his chief minister.

WINTERTIME: COLD, SCARED, HUNGRY, AND SICK

*

HOWLING STORMS. Nerve-wracking cries and smoke from their unseen neighbors in the woods. Too much cold and too little food were making people sick, probably from flu, pneumonia, tuberculosis, and scurvy. Richard Britteridge and Solomon Prower died. The Allertons' baby was stillborn; soon his mother would be dead as well.

On a grim Christmas Day, Master Jones shared out some of the *Mayflower's* beer. (The colonists' supply was gone.) Elder Brewster and the members of his Leyden fellowship knew of no Bible verses about Jesus's birthday being the 25th of December, so, as they saw things, why would any pure Christian mess with some holly-jolly, pagan affair? They spent the day cutting timber.

1624

George Fox, *future founder of the Society of Friends, a.k.a. Quakers, is born.*

English poet **John Donne** *writes, "No man is an island... never seek to know for whom the bell tolls; it tolls for thee."*

1625

As **Myles Standish** *discovers when he travels there, thousands of Londoners are dying of plague, and a fever kills 58-year-old* **King James I.** *Long live 24-year-old* **King Charles I** *(see 1649).*

People well enough to stand lugged stones and sawed planks and timbers. They tramped for miles, always on the lookout for possible attackers, to cut and carry thatch (dry grasses or reeds) for the roofs of the common house and their frame cottages. (Not until 1638 would Swedish colonists bring the idea of log cabins to America.) On the north bank of a brook, 19 houses, measuring about 14 by 18 feet, would line a street, New England's very first. It ran to Burial Hill, as it's known now. To Myles, it was Fort Hill, where he and the others would toil away, leveling out a place for a fortress. That was the plan.

Not until March 21 were there enough houses for the last of the *Mayflower's* passengers to move to Plymouth. Of course, by then, there weren't nearly so many Pilgrims, poor souls.

They counted six deaths in December. Myles Standish and Elder Brewster were two of the very few well enough to care for the people who were dying all around them. They built fires, made beds, and fixed what food there was to fix. The tough, red-headed soldier washed clothes and his weak, sick friends. Sturdy Myles did what he could, but he couldn't save his wife, Rose. He probably had little time to grieve for her that January when she and seven others died. William Bradford nearly died, too. That

1626

After surrounding and starving Breda's citizens for almost a year, Spanish troops grab the Dutch town and control it for the next 12 years.

Manhattan Island is purchased from Native Americans by **Peter Minuit** of the Dutch West India Company. A steal at 60 Dutch guilders (about $24).

was the month a thatched roof burned over the heads of sick folks -- and the colony's gunpowder! The sick and the well barely saved themselves and the rest of the common house.

Some days, 2 or 3 people passed away. In February, 17 in all, 13 in March, 6 more before 1621 came to an end. Myles and the others went out at night, carrying the bodies of folks who'd shared with them so much hardship. How many days and nights had they sat in that dim, stinking ship, talking about what they'd left behind and what they hoped to do? Now they lay in unmarked graves so the Indians wouldn't know how weak the colonists were; how their numbers were shrinking. The survivors stared into the dark forest, knowing it was full of eyes.

Hadn't they already been attacked? Hadn't tools been stolen? (They were returned later.) Didn't the English know by heart dreadful stories of murdered colonists? Myles Standish and Master Jones of the *Mayflower* saw to it that four cannon were dragged to the top of their big hill. They were clumsy to load, hard to aim, and as likely to blow up the gunner as the intended victim, but they did wonders for the colonists' morale. Doubtless, Captain Standish stood on his lofty gun platform, wiping his sweaty forehead and squaring his shoulders, grim and triumphant.

1626

French traders from the Compagnie Normandie build St. Louis, a settlement on Africa's Senegal River.

Philosopher/statesman **Sir Francis Bacon** conducts an experiment: preserving chickens by stuffing them with snow. He catches pneumonia and dies.

French colonists settle on the island of Madagascar, off the southeast coast of Africa.

As for his neighbors, word had traveled about these strange newcomers with their thunder-and-lightning weapons. Hadn't they taken corn? Hadn't they disturbed resting places of the dead? And didn't these native-born still remember well when that Englishman Thomas Hunt, disgraced comrade of John Smith, kidnapped their people six years ago? Oh, yes. And where did he take them? To Malaga – to a slave market in Spain – where he sold them!

Kidnapped Indians below deck on a ship bound for the slave market in Malaga, Spain

1627

Korea –
Manchu (MAN-*choo*, *people from Manchuria, north of China*) *warriors ride into Korea. The Koreans stay loyal to China's emperor, whose Ming dynasty is weakening after ruling the land for 259 years (see 1644).*

India –
Shah Jahan, *son of* **Jahangir,** *newly dead Mogul emperor, begins his reign by killing male relatives who might challenge him.*

CHAPTER FIVE

Contact!

MEETING THE NEIGHBORS

✳

O N FEBRUARY 17, 1621, just as Myles was officially made "Captain-General" of the tiny Pilgrim army (his job for the next 40 years), the surprised colonists looked off to the south, beyond the brook, and saw two men making hand signals up on Strawberry Hill. Indians!

Were they wanting to talk? Captain Standish made what he hoped were agreeable gestures, then he and Stephen Hopkins, armor glinting, swords clanking, went to meet the neighbors. Myles and Hopkins laid down a musket in the grass to show that they were peaceful, but the Indians vanished. From

1628

For more than a year the Huguenots (Protestants) have held off the forces of the French crown (Catholics) from La Rochelle, their besieged stronghold in western France. At last, they surrender.

John Bunyan, *future author of Pilgrim's Progress, is born.*

Dutch troops occupy the islands of Java and the Moluccas.

beyond the hill came the sound of many running feet. Oh yes, everybody was curious, suspicious, nerves on edge.

Myles ordered every healthy man to take turns on guard duty at night. John Billington, whose boy had shot the musket on the *Mayflower*, cussed the Captain and flat refused to leave his warm bed to stand around in the middle of the night, losing shut-eye on account of any blankety-blank Indians. Furious Myles hauled him in front of a court of all the colonists. Governor John Carver, once a well-to-do London merchant, would be the judge. He ruled that the troublemaker must have his neck and heels tied together as a punishment for his disobedience. When Billington calmed down and promised to be good, kindhearted Carver let him off with a warning. How Myles must have fumed!

Years later, Plymouth fellows fought, then went their separate ways. But one of the quarrelers watched out for the other man and shot him down. The murderer was caught and sentenced to hang on September 30, 1630. It would be the first of the very few death sentences handed out in Plymouth. And who was the man at the end of the rope? None other than cranky John Billington.

1628

1629

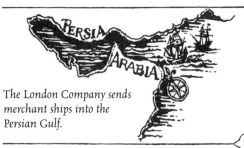

The London Company sends merchant ships into the Persian Gulf.

The painter **Peter Paul Rubens** *is sent from his home in Flanders, a region along Belgium's border with France, on a diplomatic mission to London. There he is knighted by* **Charles I.** *This is a busy year for the king. He grants a charter to the Massachusetts Bay Colony and shuts down the contrary Parliament.*

SPRING

✴

IT WAS ALMOST MARCH 25, NEW YEAR'S DAY, according to their Old Style, Julian calendar: time for the Pilgrims' annual elections. The wind had warmed. Birds were singing as a tall man came out of the forest and walked right up to the Common House. Around his waist was a fringe of leather; he carried a bow and two arrows. He raised one of his hands and spoke to the haggard, alarmed, astonished colonists.

"Welcome," he said, then he asked for some beer.

* * *

Samoset was a Pemaquid *sagamore* (chief) from up north in a place called Pemaquid Point, Maine. The Pilgrims offered him food, "strong water" (which might have been brandy or gin), and a coat, in case he got chilly. In return, they got many a question answered.

Rome –
The brilliant **Giovanni Lorenzo Bernini**, *31, sculptor (he'll sculpt Rome's most glorious fountains), writer, architect, and painter, gets the job of completing St. Peter's Cathedral.*

Mumtaz Mahal, *favorite wife of* **Shah Jahan,** *dies. For her tomb, the Mogul emperor will have built one of the most beautiful tombs the world has ever known. The Taj Mahal still stands in Agra, India.*

Samoset had learned their language from English sailors and had come to Cape Cod less than a year ago with Captain Thomas Dermer, dead now from many an arrow. Samoset was visiting with Ousemequin (Yellow Feather), also known as Massasoit (Great Leader) of the Wampanoag (People of the First Light).

He told the Englishmen that it had been Nauset warriors who attacked them that morning in December, and the folks who had lived here were Patuxet people. To them the little bay was known as Accomack. Back in the years between 1616 and 1618, sickness had killed the Patuxets. (Many a ship brought death to Native Americans, who had no immunity to European diseases such as measles and scarlet fever.) No need to fear that others might take this land, haunted perhaps with evil spirits, from the colonists. What glances must've been exchanged between folks who'd been burying friends for weeks!

After spending the night in Stephen Hopkins's well-guarded house, Samoset left, with presents from the colonists. They hoped that he would come back, with furs to trade. He did return, bringing with him beaver pelts and five tall braves who sang and danced -- on a Sunday! Not a day on which the Pilgrims could do business, they explained as tactfully as they could.

1630

Buccaneers take Tortuga in the West Indies and make it their hideaway.

Paris, France — Lemonade is invented.

TISQUANTUM, A.K.A. SQUANTO

✳

IT WAS SAMOSET'S VISIT ON MARCH 22 that would mean the most to Plymouth Colony. With him was a remarkable survivor, Tisquantum, just about the last of the Patuxets of Accomack. Taken to England by Captain Weymouth when he was barely out of his teens, he translated for Captain John Smith on his New England voyage in 1614, then was kidnapped (along with 19 other Patuxets and 7 Nausets) by the notorious Captain Hunt and sold into slavery in Spain.

Some of his kinsmen ended up in North Africa, but Tisquantum was taken in by *friars* (monks) hoping to convert him to Christianity. Somehow he wound up first in the home of a London merchant then in Newfoundland, where Governor John Mason hooked Tisquantum up with Thomas Dermer, who wanted to explore Cape Cod Bay. They did, but only after the two

---

Anne Dudley Bradstreet sets out from England for the New World, where she will become America's first great poet.

John Winthrop and 1,000 Puritan settlers arrive in Massachusetts Bay and begin a settlement that will become the city of Boston.

Powerful military leader and charismatic statesman **King Gustavus Adolphus** of Sweden goes with his troops to fight on the side of German Protestants (see 1632).

of them sailed to England to visit that booster for New England colonization, Sir Ferdinando Gorges.

Another Atlantic crossing. "I arrived," Captain Dermer wrote in 1619, "at my savage's native country (finding all dead)."

Now here was 36-year-old Tisquantum, also known as Squanto, in his native Accomack, about to become the Pilgrims' friend and teacher and a hero in the history of Europe's colonization of North America. Squanto was, as far as William Bradford was concerned, "a special instrument of God." He saved the colonists from starving to death.

The newcomers' main survival skills were endurance and determination. By the sea, in a land teeming with life, they knew beans about hunting, gathering, and fishing. And maybe they weren't the only folks in the world to be picky, at first, about eating what they weren't used to, wishing instead for good old English bread, cheese, beef, and beer.

One day, Samoset and Squanto brought astonishing news: Massasoit was nearby. He'd come 40 miles, all the way from Sowams (at Rhode Island's Narragansett Bay), and he wanted to talk. Might the colonists choose an ambassador to arrange a meeting with Massasoit, great leader of the Wampanoag people?

1631

1632

The 30-ton sloop *Blessing of the Bay, the first American-built ship, is launched into Boston harbor.*

William Claiborne *opens a trading post on Kent Island in Chesapeake Bay.*

Jan Vermeer, *future brilliant painter, is born in Holland.*

John Locke *is born in England. His writings about liberty will have a big effect on the ideals of the American republic.*

Massasoit with some of his Wampanoag warriors

A very tall, dignified man stood silent on the hilltop south of the brook, his face dyed mulberry red, his body oiled and gleaming. He wore a deerskin, a knife, and a chain of white bone beads. Imagine the tattered colonists staring at such a visitor. They must have been even more astounded as 60 grim warriors appeared beside the great chief.

Only a day after his wife, Elizabeth, died, Edward Winslow, 25-year-old former printer, set out on his first of many diplomatic missions in the New World. He brought Massasoit two knives, a copper chain, butter, and biscuits. Winslow offered him "strong water," too, which sent sweat pouring down the chief's face.

Gustavus Adolphus, *37, is killed in battle. His 6-year-old daughter,* **Christina**, *is named Queen of Sweden. As soon as she is 18, she'll run the country — for a while (see 1654).*

Lord Baltimore *is granted territory in Maryland, where Roman Catholics and folks of other faiths are free to settle.*

The American Indian World Before European Contact

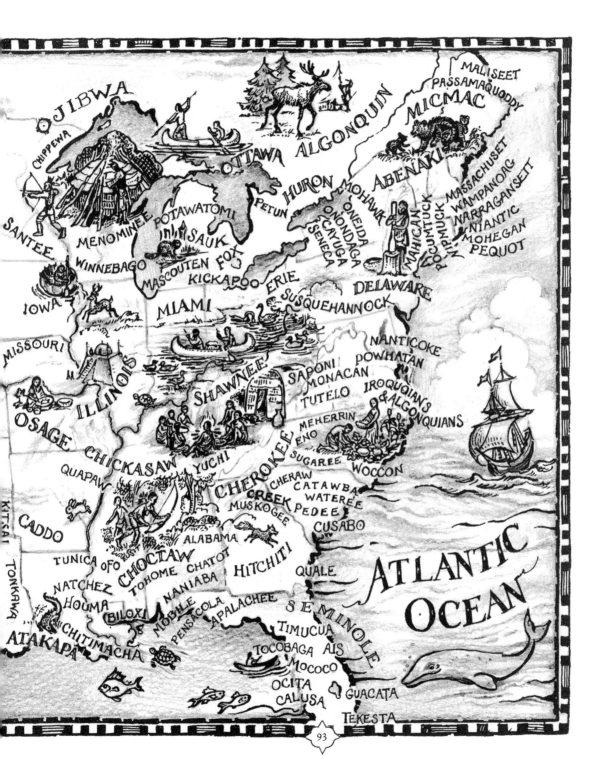

Winslow stayed with the chief's brother, Quadequina, and 40 braves beyond the brook as Massasoit and 20 warriors entered Plymouth. Captain Standish, Elder Brewster, and a 6-musketeer guard of honor saluted their visitors and conducted them past goggle-eyed Pilgrim kids to a half-finished house. Massasoit and the more important men were seated on a green rug and some cushions where they waited to meet the chief of the colonists.

Myles saw to it that musket bearers as well as a man beating a drum and another playing a fanfare on the trumpet marched into the house ahead of Governor John Carver. The two chiefs drank to each other. With the help of Samoset and Squanto, they made a treaty between their peoples that very day. They promised not to hurt each other. If harm was done, the offender would be punished by his or her own people. The natives and the new-comers promised not to steal anything from each other. If this happened, the taker would return the stolen object to its owner. They agreed to help each other. If either side was attacked unjustly, the other side would come to the rescue. When visiting, the men agreed to leave their muskets, bows, and arrows at a safe distance. The treaty lasted 40 years, until the death of Massasoit.

1633

Rome –
Galileo *is judged by the ministers of the Inquisition and given a choice: Be tortured on the rack or take back what he's said about Earth spinning around the Sun. At this time in the world, this goes against the official teachings of the Roman Catholic Church. The old scientist gives in, but he spends the rest of his life near Florence, under house arrest.*

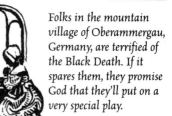

Folks in the mountain village of Oberammergau, Germany, are terrified of the Black Death. If it spares them, they promise God that they'll put on a very special play.

ANOTHER FAREWELL

*

THE TIME HAD COME. Because so many of his crew had died and some were still so weak, and because the weather was so rotten and his former passengers were in such a bad way, the skipper had stayed longer than he'd intended. Now Master Jones was getting ready to sail back to England — without any furs or timber for Mr. Weston and the other moneymen. These investors would have to wait a while longer. Away went the *Mayflower* on the pearly morning of April 5, 1621, after many tearful farewells and exchanges of real affection and respect.

No one tried to catch a ride back. Saint or Stranger, they all stayed put, united. This was home. They'd paid for it with a boatload of suffering and courage. Still, did their breath catch in their throats as their only link with the old, known world disappeared over the horizon?

1634

The people of Oberammergau put on their first "Passion Play" about the death and resurrection of Jesus. They'll perform it every decade for the next 400 years.

Jean Nicolet *travels by canoe on Lake Huron and beyond. It's such a long trip, he expects to meet the emperor of China, but no. On the edge of Lake Michigan, at today's Green Bay, Wisconsin, he meets the Menominee people.*

It took the *Mayflower* less than half the time to cross the ocean this time, thanks to the Gulf Stream, an ocean current that would be mapped and named by Ben Franklin more than a hundred years in the future. The ship got to London on the 6th of May, 1621. Ten months later, Christopher Jones was in his grave. America was mighty hard on him. On everybody.

Meanwhile back in Plymouth, Edward Winslow and Susanna White, mother of baby Peregrine and his big brother, had each lost their partners to the winter sickness. Now, on the 12th of May, theirs was Plymouth Colony's very first wedding. Was it a sign that better times were coming?

LEARNING THE LAND

✳

WHAT DID SQUANTO TEACH THE PILGRIMS? How to better live off the land; how to squish fat eels — good eating! — out of muddy

1634

Dutchman **Harmen Meyndertsz van den Bogaert** *treks into the wilderness that is today's New York State. He brings back accounts of the Mohawks' way of life.*

Dutch folks go nuts for tulips, trading fortunes for a single bulb. All of these prized, delightful flowers came from one ancestor: a tulip brought to Vienna, Austria, from Turkey back in the 1500s.

riverbanks with their feet. Most importantly, they learned when and how to plant the seed corn: Bury five kernels and three *alewives* (herrings) in each hillock. Twenty acres equaled over 96,000 hillocks to be weeded and watched so wolves wouldn't come eat those 288,000 fish. Where on earth would they catch them? Squanto told the bewildered English to wait and see. The fish swarmed the brook every spring, and there they were, right on schedule. Squanto showed the colonists how to trap them and how to gather fish manure. They lugged basket after basket of this good fertilizer and buckets of water out to the fields and gardens.

Every day but Sunday, the Pilgrims, still winter-weak, tended the precious corn and did their other endless tasks. It was too much for John Carver. He came in from the hot sun, fell into a coma and died. (Weeks later, his wife, Catherine, died, too.) The 50 survivors, less than half their original number, chose 31-year-old William Bradford to be the new governor. He was still weak from the winter sickness that had nearly killed him, so they elected an assistant governor: Isaac Allerton.

Think of Plymouth Colony as a little country, with William Bradford its new president. One of the first things he did (when he wasn't weeding corn with Myles, secretary of defense) was

1635

The Ottoman Turks invade Persia.	On the island of Great Britain, overland postal service begins as a small mail coach sets off on the road between London, England, and Edinburgh, Scotland.		Boston – North America's first high school is begun.

send Edward Winslow, secretary of state, along with ambassadors Squanto and Stephen Hopkins, out in the shallop to make peace with folks of other nations and cement trade relations.

In July, on their way to Wampanoag headquarters at Sowams, these pioneer diplomats wowed the Namaskets by blasting a corn-eating crow out of the sky. At Massasoit's house, their host agreed to stop his people from visiting Plymouth so much. He told them about the hostile Narragansetts across the bay and about the great sickness. The plague that had hit Squanto's tribe had killed thousands of the Wampanoags as well. Sad it was and shocking to Winslow and the others to see skulls and bones still unburied about the countryside.

Massasoit sent Hobomok, one of his most valued warriors, to go with the English on their return journey, as sort of a personal ambassador. Hobomok ended up staying with them for the rest of his life, becoming, in fact, part of Myles Standish's household. In August, Squanto, Governor Bradford, and a Pilgrim posse climbed into the shallop and set off on a rescue mission. The son of cranky John Billington, brother of the kid who was playing with gunpowder on the *Mayflower*, got himself lost in the woods. John Jr. wound up miles away, out on the Cape with the Nausets. Their chief and

1636

A handful of settlements combine to form the colony of Connecticut, a.k.a. the River Colony.

Roger Williams, *run out of Massachusetts because he wanted more religious freedom, begins Providence, Rhode Island's first colonial settlement, on land he got from the Narragansetts.*

Young John Billington's summer adventure

a hundred braves met Bradford not far from where some of them had attacked him and Myles and the others that icy morning in December, right after they'd arrived. Now, on a summer evening, they made peace. And a swap: The tribe got paid for the corn dug out of their hilltop. The colonists got the kid.

Was that the end of the summer's adventures? Certainly not. Governor Bradford got alarming news: Massasoit captured

Massachusetts – A college is begun. It will be named after **John Harvard**, a Puritan minister.

Dutch folks settle on Ceylon (see 1612) and on Manhattan Island, where they begin the town of Haarlem.

Japan's shogun **Tokugawa Iemitsu** forbids his people to leave their land.

by the Narragansetts! Really, it was only a rumor, but who knew? If their friend was in trouble, then the colonists had to help him. As Captain Standish began readying his tiny army for possible battle with Massasoit's captors, Squanto and Hobomok hurried south to find out what was up — only to be attacked themselves.

At Nemasket, a Pocasset chief named Corbitant pulled knives on the two of them and threatened to kill Squanto! (Without Squanto the translator, these English wouldn't be able to go around getting cosy with everybody, messing up the balance of power.) Hobomok fought his way free, and next thing you know, he, Myles, and about a dozen other men were on the march. By golly, if they lost Squanto, Corbitant would lose his head, by order of Governor Bradford!

Soon the summer night around Corbitant's village went from quiet to chaos as muskets boomed, their flashes lighting up the trees. Screaming! Dogs barking! Myles shouting, as he and his men charged into Corbitant's hut. They found Squanto alive and safe, but Corbitant? He had escaped.

Very well. Fine. Just the same, Myles made a stern speech to the Pocassets: Corbitant had better stop stirring up trouble, and Massasoit had better get home safe — or else. After all this ruckus,

1637

Mystic, Connecticut – A horrible revenge for deadly Pequot raids: English settlers, Mohegans, and Narragansetts attack a fort and kill the Pequots inside — more than 500 men, women, and children.		Civil war – Two families, the **Trinh** and the **Nguyen,** have been fighting for decades for control of the land which will be known as Vietnam.

things were a lot calmer, for a while. Massasoit was indeed safe among his people. Corbitant did quiet down, but he made sure to keep plenty of distance between himself and the people of Plymouth Colony.

A month later, Myles, Squanto, and ten other men sailed north in search of more allies and trading partners. They came to an admirably deep harbor with many islands and a peninsula called Shawmut. Myles wished they'd settled here! But no, nine years off in the future, this was where English Puritans would begin the town of Trimountaine. They dropped this name later on, and the village became known as Boston.

Myles and the other men met a group of ladies of the Massachusetts tribe. Draped around their shoulders were glossy beaver skins. On hearing that the English were in the market for such furs, the women took them off, there and then, modestly covering themselves with leafy branches.

Captain Standish's face must've been plenty red that day!

1638

French traders explore the Senegal River in western Africa.

The Dutch economy takes a beating as the tulip trade collapses.

Nagasaki, Japan — Thousands of peasants who had risen up and rebelled against the harsh rule of **Iemitsu** are destroyed by his army.

Border text (clockwise from top): VENISON * BOILED SALLET (VEGETABLES & GREENS) * PARSNIPS * BEETS * COD * BASS * PUDDINGS * BERRY TARTS * ROASTED DUCKS, GEESE, * SWANS or TURKEYS * CHEESE * ONIONS * CORN * BREAD * EELS

CHAPTER SIX

Making Room at the Table

THE FIRST THANKSGIVING

*

THINGS WERE LOOKING UP. Thanks to a summer's worth of diplomacy and hard work, friendships, trade, and crops had flourished. Well, not so much the English peas, wheat, and barley — travel was hard on seeds, too — but the American corn was great. Most everybody felt better now, and stronger, with food in their bellies. They began getting their houses snug for winter. Thankful was what they were, for all of this, for their neighbors, and for having survived.

Governor Bradford sent four men out to hunt for birds "so we might, after a special manner, rejoice together after we had

1638

Turks grab Baghdad from the Persians and make the old city part of the Ottoman Empire.

Anne Hutchinson is ordered out of Massachusetts because of her religious beliefs. Her family and followers form settlements in Rhode Island.

gathered the fruit of our labors." It was time for celebrating the ripening of the crops, for Harvest Home, for feasting in the fall of the year as people had done since ancient times all around the world. Nowadays, this autumn gathering is called Thanksgiving.

The feast lasted three days. Imagine bright trees, woodsmoke, and women stirring bubbling kettles. Meat roasting on spits over open fires. Kids running around. Lots of company, including Massasoit and 90 of his men.

Massasoit's hunters contributed five deer to the menu, which probably included boiled or grilled cod and bass, eels, and ducks, geese, swans, and "Turkies." Corn cakes and skillet breads. English *sallets* (vegetables) such as beets, parsnips, cabbage, onions, radishes, turnips, and carrots. The colonists had probably become acquainted with these American foods: chestnuts, walnuts, and hickory nuts, squash, beans, watercress, and roasted corn. There and then, they wouldn't have had potatoes. Pumpkins, perhaps, but not in the sort of pies we're used to. More likely, dried cherries, plums, or berries were steamed and/or baked in crusts or puddings.

Since the barley crop hadn't done very well, there might not have been much beer, but the colonists made red and white wine

1638 1639

Swedish folks build Delaware's first permanent settlement. They name Fort Christina after their queen (see 1632).

Fighting starts up between Presbyterians in Scotland and forces of the king and the Church of England.

Cambridge, Massachusetts – North America gets its first printing press.

from wild grapes. No coffee, no tea. Food was eaten with knives and fingers, so big, linen napkins were kept handy. There weren't any forks and not too many spoons.

When they weren't eating or sleeping, what did they do for three days? No football and no televisions. But stoolball? Absolutely! The colonists loved this ball-bat-and-wicket game, which was sort of a pioneer version of croquet. How about foot races? Wrestling matches? Men and boys showing off their shooting? Amazing archery? Oh yes, lots of all of these, and plenty of singing and dancing, too.

Massasoit and his men were delighted to see how well Myles handled a bow and arrow, and that wasn't all Captain Standish did. He led his best troops in a military parade. Then, up on Fort Hill, he showed off what a wonderful, appalling CRASH his biggest cannon could make! Imagine people squinching up their eyes and putting hands over their ears, birds fluttering up in clouds out of the treetops, and wide-eyed warriors.

The little red-headed Captain Standish loved making a big impression.

A fine time was had by all, and you might imagine that all would go smoothly now for Plymouth Colony. You'd be wrong.

1640

Violence breaks out in France, as peasants revolt against heavy taxes.

Because he needs money for his war against the Scots **King Charles I** *opens Parliament for the first time since 1629, dismisses the lawmakers, then calls them back. This "Long Parliament" stays in session for a, well, long time (see 1653).*

SAILS!

✳

ON NOVEMBER 11, 1621, A SENSATIONAL SIGHT appeared on the horizon: sails! They belonged to the *Fortune*. On board were 35 hungry new colonists, unexpected company late for dinner. The *Fortune*'s crew needed food, too, for their return voyage. In no time, Plymouth's cupboards were dangerously empty, and Governor Bradford's mind was full of worries.

On top of having to put everybody on half rations, he had to think about what had come in the *Fortune*'s mail pouch: a pretty hot letter from Mr. Weston. He and the other moneymen were mad. Had they gotten anything in return for their investment? Where were the furs? Where was all that good American timber? (England's forests were going or gone.)

Bradford bristled. Were there not graves full of those who had given their lives for this colony? Hadn't they themselves invested

---

1640   **1641**

Death of **Peter Paul Rubens**. His brilliant student, **Anton Van Dyck**, the age's best-known portrait painter, will die next year.

After 60 years, Portugal gets out from under Spain's control.

Irish folk rise up against their wealthy, mostly English landlords. Nearly 10,000 Protestants are killed, and the English are driven out of Ulster in northern Ireland (see 1649).

all their suffering and hard labor under impossible conditions?

The men of Plymouth loaded the ship with lumber and pelts. If only pirates hadn't captured the unfortunate *Fortune*. If only they hadn't swiped her cargo, the colonists might have paid back much of what they owed, but no. They were still deep, deep in debt.

FRESH TROUBLES

✳

IN JANUARY 1622, ANOTHER SURPRISE showed up at Plymouth — an ugly one. The Narragansetts' leader, Canonicus, sent a bunch of arrows, nicely gift-wrapped in a rattlesnake skin. Governor Bradford answered this challenge with one of his own: the same skin stuffed with shot and gunpowder. It worked. Just one look at this skinful of musket ammo about scared the chief to death. But, back at Plymouth, the governor and his "secretary of defense" weren't taking any chances. When Myles Standish

1642

English lawmakers get rid of the detested "Star Chamber" where **Charles I** had confessions tortured out of his enemies and/or had them tried without a jury.

Dutch navigator **Abel Janszoon Tasman** is the first European to set foot briefly on the island of New Zealand, where fierce **Maori** warriors do NOT put out the welcome mat!

and the others weren't out patrolling, they were hard at work on a strong, tall *palisade* (a fence of saplings, the tops pointed sharp) all around the colony. If they felt any safer, they didn't feel that way for long.

In June, some fishermen brought shocking news from Virginia and a load of fresh fear to Plymouth. Dateline: March 22, 1622. Jamestown Settlement. Native warriors kill 347 colonists! (This attack sparked years of war in which a multitude of Powhatan people died.)

When they heard this terrible news from Jamestown, the Plymouth folks lost whatever sense of safety they'd had. They must protect themselves. The colony must have a fortress! Soon, Myles and the others were breaking their backs, chopping and dragging logs to the top of their big hill. They sawed, hammered, and built. Before another year passed, the little captain could stand up there, grim and proud, looking out over land and sea, from a fort every bit as sturdy as he. It was a fortress, jail, courthouse, town hall, and meetinghouse combined, in which Elder Brewster preached fine sermons. Earnest faith, thick walls, good cannon, and tough Captain Standish: God willing, they could be counted on to keep the colonists safe from all harm.

1642

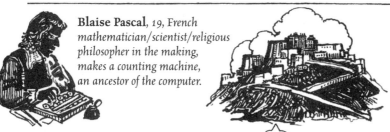

Blaise Pascal, 19, *French mathematician/scientist/religious philosopher in the making, makes a counting machine, an ancestor of the computer.*

Ngawang Losang Gyatso, *the Dalai Lama, is Tibet's spiritual leader and as of this year, the head of its government. Workers are finishing his mountaintop monastery: the Palace of Potala.*

WHAT DID THEY WEAR?

They liked good strong colors: reds, yellows, greens, blues, and russet (reddish-brown) as well as gray, brown, and respectable black. Women and girls wore linen coifs (caps). Indoors and out, men and boys wore their hats. The English colonists wore long-sleeved linen garments under their wool or linen outer clothes.

separate collar

waistcoat

pocket

apron

skirt

doublet

coif

breeches

Ribbons held up folks' stockings which were made of cloth or — more up-to-date — knitted.

It had been another tough year marked with a puny harvest, misunderstandings, jealousies, illness, battle, and death. Myles, Massasoit, and Tisquantum: all three got sick, and only two got well. Squanto, who'd survived so much, died in the fall of 1622, asking his friend William Bradford to pray that he might "go to ye Englishmen's God in heaven."

For his part, Mr. Weston, the adventurer, sent more trouble to Plymouth. Besides writing letters, he sent people along, fully expecting that the Plymouth folks would help them out. Though Mr. Weston had given up on the Pilgrims, these new folks would be planting his colony up at Wessagusset (now Weymouth).

These Wessagusset men were an unruly bunch as well as corn thieves, and they were hot competition for Plymouth colonists' totally necessary fur trade with their native-born neighbors. As if all this weren't bad enough, these new colonists began stirring up trouble with the Massachusetts tribe, particularly the warrior Wituwamet, who was growing more and more fed up with all these English folks. Boatload after boatload of them kept coming. Among his people, Wituwamet began fanning bad feelings into flames.

Soon Captain Standish, Hobomok, and the other Pilgrim

1642

1643

December 25 –
Future scientist,
Isaac Newton,
is born in England.

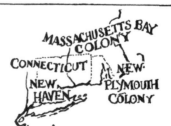

New Plymouth,
Massachusetts Bay, New
Haven, and Connecticut
form themselves into the
United Colonies of New
England.

commandos were on the march. Their mission? A peacemaking raid on the Massachusetts. By the time all was said and done, the Wessagusset men took off for Maine or back across the Atlantic, seven Massachusetts people were killed, and the grim little captain returned to Plymouth carrying a bloody war trophy: the head of Wituwamet. For years thereafter, many a summer, fall, winter, and spring, Myles's trophy decorated a spike on the walls of the fortress, high on the hill over Plymouth Colony. It was a nasty old custom. Many a troublesome person had his severed head displayed as a warning. Birds pecked out many an eyeball, and skulls grinned down, their sightless eyes staring out upon 17th-century London and plenty of other places.

Way over in Holland, the Saints' old pastor John Robinson heard about the killings. It might be glorious in some men's eyes, but it did not please God. It was not proper for Christians "to be a terror to poor, *barbarous* [uncivilized] people."

You will say they deserved it, but, the pastor wondered, weren't the Indians provoked? "You're no judges over them," he said, and he asked them to consider Captain Standish's personality. It was, perhaps, wanting "tenderness."

Perhaps.

Louis XIII *dies. Thanks to his late prime minister,* **Cardinal Richelieu,** *he leaves behind a strong France and a strong monarchy. The new king is a little boy, so his mom,* **Anne of Austria,** *and* **Cardinal Mazarin** *(see 1648) will run things for a while.* **Louis XIV** *will reign for the next 72 years.*

1623: TWO SHIPS, TWO BRIDES, AND A MIRACLE

*

FROM THE BEGINNING, THE MONEYMEN in England insisted that the colony's crop lands should belong, in common, to everybody. This kind of planned economy sounded good on paper, but it doesn't always work so well with real individuals, as many would discover in Russia and other places in the distant 20th century. Governor Bradford thought there'd be more food raised and folks would work better if each family had their own bit of land. He was right, but oh, if only it would rain!

Plymouth's Town Brook shrank to a trickle that summer of 1623. The colonists' gardens wilted along with their spirits, and their cheeks flushed red with heat. The fields were so, so dry. In the middle of that hot, dusty summer, two ships, the *Anne* and the *Little James*, arrived, bringing family members and church friends.

1643

1644

Religious leader **Anne Hutchinson** *and her family are attacked and killed by native neighbors after moving to Long Island (now part of New York).*

Bejing –
After 276 years, a dynasty ends in China. The last Ming emperor hangs himself rather than let himself be captured as Manchu rule begins. It'll last until 1912.

Soon the colony was bubbling with happy reunions. Two of the Plymouth men were particularly happy to greet a pair of the lady passengers, but more about them later. The new folks were sad — shocked really — to see how tattered and skinny the Old Comers were, those ragged veterans of the *Mayflower* and the *Fortune*. Soon enough they realized their shared danger: If rain did not come to water their crops, they would face a starvation winter. All of the colonists, old and new alike, joined together in a special day of prayer. The sun beat down upon them, and the dry grasses crisped under their feet as they gathered to pray for rain.

They prayed all day. Picture them that afternoon, their faces turned up to watch clouds gathering gray and heavy, filling up the sky. Imagine a freshening wind bending the treetops. The first cold drops, plopping and spattering. Curtains of rain and that sweet smell coming up from the thirsty earth. It was a time for rejoicing -- and another festival.

That "first Thanksgiving" in 1621 had to have been bittersweet, so soon after so many deaths. The harvest was mighty thin in the year that followed, but 1623 — now there was a year! Reunited families, a miraculous rain, a saved corn crop: If all of this was cake, two weddings were the frosting.

Antonio Stradivari,
future maker of violins,
is born in Italy.

William Penn,
future Quaker colo-
nizer of Pennsylvania,
is born in England.

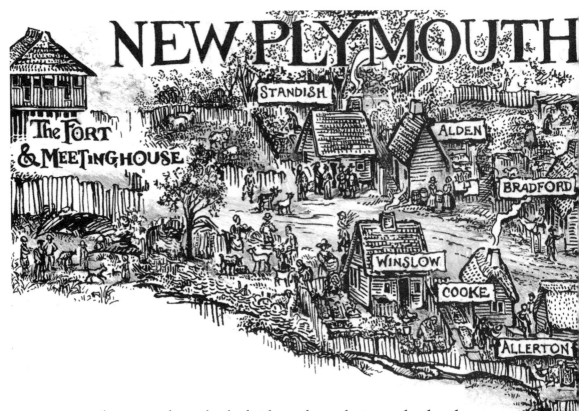

NEW PLYMOUTH

THE FORT & MEETINGHOUSE

STANDISH
ALDEN
BRADFORD
WINSLOW
COOKE
ALLERTON

The *Fortune* brought the brides-to-be to their new husbands in America. Governor Bradford married Alice Southworth, a young widow. Barbara was the second bride. Her last name is lost in the mists of the past. The name she got after she married, we know very well: Mrs. Myles Standish. How Myles and Barbara

1644   **1645**

July 2 –
Oliver Cromwell's *Roundheads crush* **King Charles I's** *Cavaliers at the Battle of Marston.*

The Cavaliers are defeated again and again in England's Civil War.

July 12 –
Czar Mikhail Romanov, *is dead at 49. His 16-year-old son,* **Alexis Mikhailovich,** *will rule Russia – harshly.*

met no one knows, but some say that the bride's older sister was Rose, Myles's first wife.

Massasoit, wearing the skin of a black wolf, brought his main wife (four others stayed home) as well as some other chiefs and 120 warriors to this carnival of food, dancing, and good cheer. For the governor and Alice, for Myles Standish and his bride, what a day it must have been!

1646

German scientist **Athanasius Kircher** *is inventing a magic lantern to project pictures on a wall.*

Peter Stuyvesant, *minus a leg he'd lost in battle, becomes the last Dutch governor of New Netherland (New York).*

Captain Standish delivers a report to the other leaders of Plymouth.

CHAPTER SEVEN

The Business of Life & Death

GOOD NEWES/BAD NEWES

*

WHEN THE *ANNE* SAILED BACK TO LONDON, she was loaded with lots of New England timber plus furry bales of beaver and otter pelts. Edward Winslow went along, too, intent on meeting with the moneymen and getting his book printed. It would be called: *Good Newes from New-England* or *A true relation of things very remarkable at the Plantation of Plimoth.* It wasn't his first book about Plymouth Colony. He and William Bradford had written an earlier one. The manuscript was one of the few things the French buccaneers didn't steal when they attacked the *Fortune.* Because it was published by someone called G. Mourt,

1646

The king's Cavaliers lose to the Parliamentarian Roundheads, and Civil War ends in England.

Swedish and French troops invade Bavaria (Germany).

Sir Thomas Browne, an English doctor, coins the term "electricity."

Bradford's and Winslow's book is known as *Mourt's Relation.* (Here, "relation" means "story.")

The reason for writing these books was, of course, to earn money and teach people about America, especially potential investors in New World colonies. Working out colonial business, paying off the money the colonists owed: These things were every bit as difficult as growing corn and catching fish. Only a few years after the *Fortune* was raided, another ship, the *Little James,* was grabbed by Barbary pirates, and the Pilgrims' money problems became even worse.

Isaac Allerton sailed to England more than once, trying to improve the colony's financial agreements. So did Myles Standish, in 1625, but neither man was very good at business. When Myles returned from London, he was loaded down with news and lucky to be alive. An epidemic was raging. More than 40,000 Londoners died that year from that cruel old plague, the Black Death. And Myles had still more news: The king was dead! Prince Charles had taken over the throne of England. (No one knew it then, but as a king, Charles would be every bit as bullheaded as his old man, King James. He'd end up sparking a civil war and getting his royal, stubborn head chopped off!)

1647

Preacher **George Fox**, *23, inspires followers. He and his Society of Friends (Quakers) will face jail and trouble from English judges and churchmen.*

Charles I *is taken prisoner by the pro-Parliament Roundhead army, escapes, and is caught again on an island in the English Channel.*

Russians rise up against **Czar Alexis**. *He will retaliate by further grinding down the poor peasants.*

For the Pilgrims, Myles's most sorrowful news of all was that the Saints' much-loved Pastor Robinson had passed away over in Leyden. Sad, sad, sadness in Plymouth, when they heard this.

The colonists' attempts at boat-building, salt-making, and fish-catching were never as successful as they hoped, but they never gave up. They raised corn and cattle, too, all descendants of three cows and a bull, New England's first livestock. It was Edward Winslow who, in 1624, brought these creatures to America. Afterwards, Winslow and a handful of other men sailed hundreds of miles into the north — a daring adventure! — up the Kennebec River, to trade Plymouth corn for valuable beaver skins. Soon the Pilgrims had a fur trading post up in present-day Maine and another, called Aptucxet, down near their own Buzzards Bay.

Fur and cattle were Plymouth's main ways of making money. Protecting these was one of Governor Bradford's main worries. When Thomas Morton, the man in charge of a settlement off to the north, began grabbing up piles of pelts, letters were exchanged between the governor of Plymouth and the master of Merry Mount.

1648

Peace —
The Treaty of Westphalia ends the Thirty Years' War. Germany is pretty much wrecked — a third of its people are dead. Spain and the Netherlands quit fighting, too.

Scots invade England. They're soundly whacked by **Oliver Cromwell**'s *pro-Parliament Roundheads.*

THE ADVENTURE OF
THE MERRY MOUNT MAYPOLE
OR HOW MYLES GOT HIS NICKNAME

✳

THOMAS MORTON WAS A WELL-EDUCATED ARISTOCRAT and, like the Saints of Leyden, he had strong ideas about how life in the New World should be. But his settlement, near the present-day town of Quincy, was very different from Plymouth Colony off to the south. Not only was he horning in on Plymouth's fur trade, he also was selling muskets to the natives and teaching them how to shoot. Myles must've blown his top when he heard about that! And Mr. Morton seemed to be offering poor indentured (see page 121) workers a way out of their servitude. Not a bad idea, to our way of thinking, but to the people of Plymouth Plantation back there in the 17th century, a haven for runaway servants would turn the colonial economy upside down.

1648

Under the harsh rule of the shogun **Iemitsu**, the Japanese people suffer and go hungry.

French nobles want back the military power they lost to the forces of the crown. This becomes a general, violent uprising known as the Fronde, from the word for the slings used for flinging rocks at **Cardinal Mazarin's** window.

On top of all of this, Master Morton of Merry Mount had set up a maypole around which people were merry indeed, drinking and "dancing...like so many fairies, or furies," according to outraged Governor Bradford. This was not the America he had in mind. Plymouth's tiny army must be sent to take care of business. Once again, in 1629, Myles Standish was on the march. Did Myles get his man? Oh, yes, but that wasn't all he got.

TO BE A SERVANT

*I*n the world of Myles Standish, most servants were indentured, meaning there was a contract: servant's work for master's food and shelter for an agreed-upon number of years. Often the edge of the actual contract was notched, or indented: indentured. The master might agree to teach a young servant a craft and/or how to read. Orphans were regularly "bound out" to masters. Servants' working papers and remaining years of service were bought and sold all the time. Now Morton had gathered up a bunch of servants, telling them that they would "trade, plant, & live together as equals." It was an idea ahead of his time, and as bold, pleasure-loving Thomas Morton quickly discovered, out of place in colonial Massachusetts.

1649

January 6 –
Louis XIV, *the boy-king of France, barely escapes forces of the* Fronde *in Paris.*

January 30 –
King Charles I *is beheaded. England will be – until 1660 anyway – a Commonwealth, a kingless republic. Plenty of royalists head to Virginia.*

Oliver Cromwell *marches his troops into Ireland to put down the uprising (see 1641).*

Myles and his band of Pilgrims went to work on the maypole with their axes. As for Mr. Morton, he ended up being shipped off to England where he wrote a very lively book, *New English Canaan*, about his time in America. In it he saddled Myles with a permanent nickname when he told of getting arrested by short, red-faced "Captaine Shrimpe" and his bumbling eight-man army. Of course it wasn't this clever rascal or even William Bradford who gave Myles his greatest fame. It was up to another writer — Henry Wadsworth Longfellow — to do that way off in the future, in 1858. More about him later.

Thomas Morton turned up back in Plymouth some years after his maypole got chopped, but that's another story, too. Even Governor Bradford, in his record of the colony, had to stop himself from going on about the fascinating Mr. Morton. "I have been too long about so unworthy a person...."

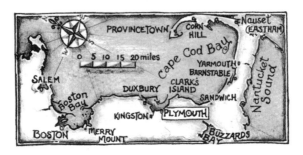

1650

From his studies of the Bible's Old Testament, **James Ussher**, an Irish archbishop, decides that the world was created October 23, 4004 B.C.

Angola –
The Portuguese win control from the Dutch and make a costly peace with warrior **Queen Nzinga Mbundu** of Ndongo and Matamba.

NEWCOMERS TO THE BAY

✳

WHERE THE SEA MET THE EASTERN SKY, more and more sails appeared as people streamed to the New World. If Thomas Morton was the most colorful competition the Pilgrims had to face, he was just one thin, very juicy slice of the pie. Off to the south, Dutch folks were settling along the Hudson River and on Manhattan Island. But the folks who'd most affect the future of Plymouth Colony were the thousands of Puritans who arrived throughout the 1620s. They settled off to the north, at Naumkeag (later known as Salem), and then on the skinny-necked Shawmut peninsula. Their settlement there became Boston, the main town of the Puritan's Massachusetts Bay Colony.

More people meant more — and more competitive — colonial business. The Plymouth folks really had to scramble. Twenty years after the *Mayflower* landed, they still owed lots of money to

The English take their first sips of tea, and in Oxford, a coffeehouse opens, England's first. Coffeehouses will be popular meeting places for serious talk.

Paris —
There's a brand-new dance going around the town:
the minuet.

ENGLAND'S CIVIL WAR 1642–1646

Like Henry VIII, King Charles I totally believed in the absolute power that went with his job. A radical idea was spreading among the commoners, especially the Puritans and lawmakers in Parliament: The king should share his power with the people. In 1642, years of arguing flamed into war between the king's Cavaliers and Parliament's army of Roundheads, so-called because of the wigless Puritans' short hair.

How did this war affect the colonists? For one thing, for a while, many Puritans fought and hoped for a better England rather than go to Massachusetts Bay. For another, this biggest, fastest growing colony in New England united, sort of, with Plymouth, New Haven, and Connecticut to protect themselves in case Dutch or French raiders bushwhacked them while their mother country was busy fighting.

After all of the brutal battles and after his trial, King Charles I had his royal head cut off in 1649. Instead of a monarchy, there was a republic in England led by stern Oliver Cromwell. It lasted until 1660, when, once again, a king sat on the English throne. And did Charles II, the "Merry Monarch," share his power with Parliament? He did.

1651

The son of dead **King Charles I** is crowned, but when **Oliver Cromwell**'s men defeat royalist troops, young **King Charles II** flees to France.

Japan – **Iemitsu** is dead. His son, **Ietsuna**, is shogun now.

In Boston – Puritans declare that observing Christmas is against the law.

the English investors. As hard as they'd worked, they'd had bitter hard luck. Hard to come by were wilderness and business skills. How would they ever get those moneymen off their backs?

Myles and six more of the colony's leaders would take charge of Plymouth's trade in furs, *wampum* (different kinds of shells used as money), milk-goats, corn, cows, etc. Then these seven "Undertakers" would *undertake* (take upon themselves) the colony's debts and pay them off, even if they had to sell some of their own properties. In the end, that's what they did, until at last, in 1645, the colony of "New Plimoth" was free and clear.

SPREADING OUT, MOVING ON

✳

BY THEN, PLYMOUTH was no longer a teeny, hardscrabble hamlet by the Town Brook. The colony's population had grown to about 3,000 souls, minus one. In the spring of 1643, William Bradford

1652

Maine territory becomes part of Massachusetts Bay Colony.

France — The Fronde *rebellion dies down. The people welcome their 14-year-old king,* **Louis XIV,** *and his mom,* **Queen Anne,** *back to Paris.*

recorded the death of 80-year-old Elder William Brewster, his "tenderhearted" friend ever since they'd met far away in Scrooby, 40 years before. Before he left his life on Earth, Elder Brewster had already gone away from the village of Plymouth, and he wasn't the only one.

It was like this: The colonists were farming folk. As growing families and their animals needed more land, new townships, such as Nauset (called Eastham nowadays), Marshfield, Taunton, Sandwich, and Rehoboth, popped up throughout Plymouth Colony. The first was Ducksburrow, or Duxburrow. (It's Duxbury now.) That's where Elder Brewster lived. So did Myles Standish.

The Standish family moved to Duxbury in 1632. Myles and Barbara probably climbed the hill there beside their house to see what they could see, they and their daughter, Lora, and their boys, Alexander, John, Myles Jr., Josiah, and Charles, the baby. When they stood on that windy hilltop and looked to the south, beyond their own thatched roof and chimney top, across the waters of the bay, they could see Plymouth. There was another member of the Standish household, too: the captain's old buddy, Hobomok. By the light of Myles's fire, might these old fighting

1652

Cape Town, South Africa, is founded by **Jan van Riebeck**.

1653

China —
Many a Europe-bound ship full of tea sets sail on the South China Sea from the port city of Amoy, which is captured by men under the command of anti-Manchu pirate **Zheng Chenkong**, a.k.a. **Koxinga**.

men have swapped stories about their battles? Old friends? What all they'd seen and done over the years before Master Jones sailed the *Mayflower* to Cape Cod Bay? If only, if only we could hear them, think what we could know.

Just knowing what we do about pioneer/explorer/builder/ nurse/farmer/grave digger/merchant/lawman/husband and dad, Myles Standish gives us plenty to admire. He was a man of vision. Almost 300 years before there was a Cape Cod Canal, it was Myles who first imagined a waterway across Cape Cod's "bicep" so people wouldn't have to sail clear around that great arm of land. He's said to have been the best in the colony when it came to speaking and understanding the language of the native-born neighbors. For many years, Myles served as an assistant to the governor of Plymouth Colony, and for a while, between 1644 to 1649, he was its treasurer too, responsible for keeping the books and collecting the taxes.

And always, Myles was a soldier. When the Narragansetts went on the warpath in 1645, Myles led a troop of 40 musketeers down to the edge of their lands, into the wilds east of the Providence River. Nine years later, when it was looking as if Dutch raiders might be on the attack, Myles assembled his

Izaak Walton *publishes* The Compleat Angler, *a peaceful classic all about going fishing.*

Former general **Oliver Cromwell,** *new "Lord Protector of England," slows down the Long Parliament. It'll formally end its session in 1660, 20 years after the late* **Charles I** *called it to order.*

troops once again. He was pushing 70 by then. Most likely, time had turned his red hair and whiskers white. The passing years had taken his son John and daughter, Lora, as well as his friend Hobomok to their graves. As it happened, a dust-up with the Dutch was avoided. Never mind. Plymouth Colony could still count on Captain Myles Standish -- but not for much longer. He got sick and died two years later, on the 3rd of October 1656.

MYLES STANDISH HAS LEFT THE BUILDING: WHAT HAPPENED THEN

*

WHAT DID MYLES LEAVE BEHIND? His Duxbury house by the hill, of course, and some Standish lands over in England. Not his "dear loving wife, Barbara," but their oldest son, Alexander, inherited these. Myles's will lists household goods, such as three brass kettles and a couple of spinning wheels. He had five horses

1654

Dutch fighters capture New Sweden (Delaware) and make it part of New Netherland. As of 1664, it'll be part of English New York.

Sweden's scholarly, 28-year-old **Queen Christina** quits her job. Disguising herself in men's clothes, she leaves the court of her Protestant country and lives out her life as a Catholic in Rome.

and a few saddles, cattle, pigs, a flock of sheep. There were his sword and cutlass as well as his guns and lots of books. You get a good idea about people if you know what they read. Consider the Standishes' bookshelves, and you might well imagine that he and some or all of his family were a thoughtful and studious bunch. And think how rare and precious books were in the middle of the 17th century! Besides Julius Caesar's book about war in ancient Gaul, the *Iliad* (about war in ancient Troy), a dictionary, and some Bibles, there were volumes on farming, law, science, medicine, *theology* (about God), and *artillery* (big weapons and how to use them). Among Myles's histories were books about Germany, Queen Elizabeth, and the nation of Turkey.

The year before Myles passed away, Edward Winslow, Pilgrim diplomat, was buried in the waters near Jamaica. He'd been on a mission to this island in the West Indies. Just seven months after Plymouth lost its steadfast Captain Jones, its long-time governor died. For 20 years, idealistic, optimistic William Bradford had been writing about "Plimoth Plantation." His 270-page manuscript had plenty of adventures of its own. It wound up in England during the American Revolution and wasn't returned to Massachusetts until 1897.

1655

Jews, recently ordered out of Portugal-controlled Brazil, arrive in New Amsterdam (now New York City).

The Swedish Army invades Poland, and Manchu warriors fight Russians in eastern Siberia.

After the great Massasoit died in 1661, things did not go at all well between the colonists, who were clearing more and more of the forests, and the Indians, who'd always hunted in the woods. And the colonists didn't deal as fairly with Massasoit's sons, Wamsutta and Metacomet (a.k.a. Alexander and "King Philip") as they had with their dad. In 1675, Philip tried to drive the English out. By 1676, his warriors were defeated; he and thousands of other Indians were in their graves. More than a thousand white settlers were dead, too, including many from Plymouth, a colony whose days were numbered.

The colonists struggled to get over King Philip's War. After 1688, they suffered through more fighting, which was all part of France and England's tug of war over America, which wouldn't end until 1763. Meanwhile, Plymouth's leaders kept up a pen-and-paper battle, trying to win for the colony a proper, official charter, something it had never had — and never would. On October 7, 1691, some 70 years after the Pilgrims' "First Thanksgiving," King William III of England made all of "New Plymouth" part of the fully chartered colony of Massachusetts Bay. Oh, yes, the islands of Nantucket and Martha's Vineyard would be part of it, too. And, until 1820, all of Maine! Boston,

1655

English troops invade Jamaica, determined to swipe this island from the Spaniards. From the sugar that's grown there, rum is made, which English sailors begin drinking instead of beer, which sours at sea.

Dutch scientist **Christian Huygens** improves telescopic lenses and discovers one each of Saturn's rings and moons. Next year he'll make the first pendulum clock.

with its fine, deep harbor that Myles Standish had admired so much, would be its capital.

Eight years later, the last of the Pilgrims passed from the Earth. Mary Allerton was four years old when she came over on the *Mayflower*. She was 83 when she died in 1699. In Plymouth.

HOW MYLES BECAME FAMOUS

MORE THAN 200 YEARS OFF IN MYLES'S FUTURE, an American poet gave him a kind of fame that would've had the old soldier shaking his head.

Henry Wadsworth Longfellow was rock-star famous himself for writing very popular story-poems like *The Song of Hiawatha* when he wrote his big hit. People in 1858 loved reading *The Courtship of Miles Standish*, a made-up story of how Myles really, really wanted Priscilla Mullins to be his wife. In the

Edmund Halley, *future astronomer, is born in England. Later on, a comet will be named after him.*

Rembrandt van Rijn, *the great painter, is broke. He puts his house and paintings up for sale.*

poem as in real life, she married John Alden. They and their 11 children were Myles's neighbors. One of the Alden girls, Sarah, married one of the Standish boys — Alexander. A high point in their town of Duxbury, Massachusetts, came to be called "Captain's Hill," because the Standish family used to live nearby. Since 1898, a stone tower has stood on top of that hill, and the tower's been crowned with a statue of Myles. There he stands, very tall. One hand is on his sword. The other is forever pointing off to Plymouth where, one long ago winter, a boat full of wanderers came to make a better world.

1657

Londoners are introduced to a new drink: hot chocolate.

1658

Amsterdam — **Jan Swammerdam,** 21, is the first to observe and describe red blood corpuscles.

1660

Sweden — The king is dead. Long live **King Charles XI.**

The Mayflower

SHE WAS A THREE-MASTED FREIGHTER, an old, sea-going truck. Master Jones and his crew had to make room for 102 people and their dogs: a big mastiff and a little spaniel. There might well have been cages populated with pigs, goats, and chickens. And almost every ship had a rat-catching cat or two. Crowded and smelly it must have been on the good ship *Mayflower*.

Where is she now? Are her timbers in a Buckingham-shire barn, as some say? Or part of a church in Oxfordshire? Perhaps. Or rotted into the bottom of the sea? After so many years, it's hard to say for certain. A splendid replica of the ship was sailed to America in 1957. At Plymouth, Massachusetts, you might climb aboard the *Mayflower* II, a present to America from the English people.

Who Sailed on the Mayflower

† *Died the first hard year, 1620–21*

Captain and Crew
(40 men, more or less)

Master Christopher Jones, part owner of the ship. Besides first mate John Clarke and second mate (or pilot) Robert Coppin, there was ship doctor Giles Heale, master's mates, a cook, a carpenter, seamen, and gunners for the ship's ten cannon. Governor Bradford wrote that "almost half of their company died before they went away [back to England]."

Leyden Saints
(17 men, 10 women, 14 children)

Isaac Allerton, a tailor in London before he came to Leyden; his wife, †Mary; their stillborn †baby; their children: Remember, Bartholomew, and 4-year-old Mary. Mary Allerton Cushman was the last of the *Mayflower* passengers to die (in 1699 in Plymouth).

William Bradford, weaver, and his wife, †Dorothy. Their 5-year-old son, John, would be nearly 12 by the time he came to America.

William Brewster, Plymouth Colony's pastor; his wife Mary, their sons, Love and Wrestling (or Wrasling). Their eldest, Jonathan, and daughters, Fear and Patience, came over later.

†John Carver, merchant, first governor of Plymouth Colony, and his wife, †Catherine (or Katherine)

Francis Cooke, a wool-comber and his boy, John

John Crackstone and his son, John, whose feet froze when got lost in the woods. He died of gangrene in 1628.

Moses Fletcher, blacksmith

Dr. Samuel Fuller, "physition & chirugeon," Deacon of the Pilgrims' Church of New Plymouth

†John Goodman, a linen weaver, who brought his two dogs along

Disire Minter. She came with the Carvers.

†Degory Priest, a hat maker from London

†Thomas Rogers, merchant, and his son, Joseph

†Edward Tilley, a weaver, and his wife, †Anne. The Tilleys brought with them two young "cousins" from London, Humility Cooper and Henry Samson. They are listed among the Strangers.

†John Tilley, a silk worker, his †wife and daughter, both named Elizabeth

†Thomas Tinker, a wood sawyer, his †wife, and †son

†William White, a wool comber (carder), and his wife, Susanna (Deacon Fuller's sister), and their 5-year-old son, Resolved. Susannah gave birth to Peregrine on board the *Mayflower*. He lived until 1704.

†John Turner and his two ††boys, all dead the first winter

Edward Winslow, a printer, and his wife, †Elizabeth

STRANGERS

John Billington, his wife, Ellen, and their boys, Francis and John, Jr. "One of ye profanest families amongst them" was the only whole family to survive the first year's general sickness.

†Richard Britteridge

Peter Browne

†James Chilton, a tailor from Canterbury, †his wife, and their teenage daughter, Mary

†Richard Clarke

Humility Cooper, a small girl from London

Francis Eaton, a carpenter and shipwright from Bristol, his wife, †Sarah, and baby, Samuel

†Edward Fuller from Norfolk, his wife, †Ann, and boy, Samuel

†Richard Gardiner, a seaman from Harwich, Essex

Stephen Hopkins, from Gloucestershire, and his wife Elizabeth, their daughters, Damaris and Constance, son, Giles. Their boy, †Oceanus, was born on the *Mayflower*.

†Edmund Margeson

†Christopher Martin, his †wife, and stepson, †Solomon Prower

†William Mullins, his wife, †Alice, their daughter, Priscilla, and little boy, †Joseph

†John Rigdale from London and his wife, †Alice

†Henry Samson of London

Captain Myles Standish and his wife, †Rose

Richard Warren, a London merchant

HIRED HANDS

John Alden, ship's cooper and future husband of Priscilla Mullins, was hired to keep the beer and water barrels snug and air-tight.

Four sailors: †John Allerton (or Alderton), a man by the name of Ely or Ellis, William Trevore, and †Thomas English, who was hired to pilot the shallop

SERVANTS

†William Butten, Samuel Fuller's servant, died at sea.

†Robert Carter worked for the Mullins family.

Dorothy (last name unknown), Mrs. Carver's maidservant

Edward Dotey. He and Edward Leister worked for Master Hopkins. These two fought Plymouth Colony's only duel!

†William Holbeck worked in the White household.

†John Hooke was perhaps Master Allerton's apprentice.

John Howland, the only heir of the childless Carvers, bought his freedom from servitude.

John Langemore worked for Christopher Martin.

William Latham, a servant boy

Edward Leister

Richard More, one of a family of young orphans put to work, a common practice. His three siblings, †Ellen, †Jasper, and another †brother, died the first winter.

George Soule from Worcestershire

†Elias Story, the Winslow's manservant from London

†Edward Thompson worked for the White family.

†Roger Wilder, a manservant in the Carver household

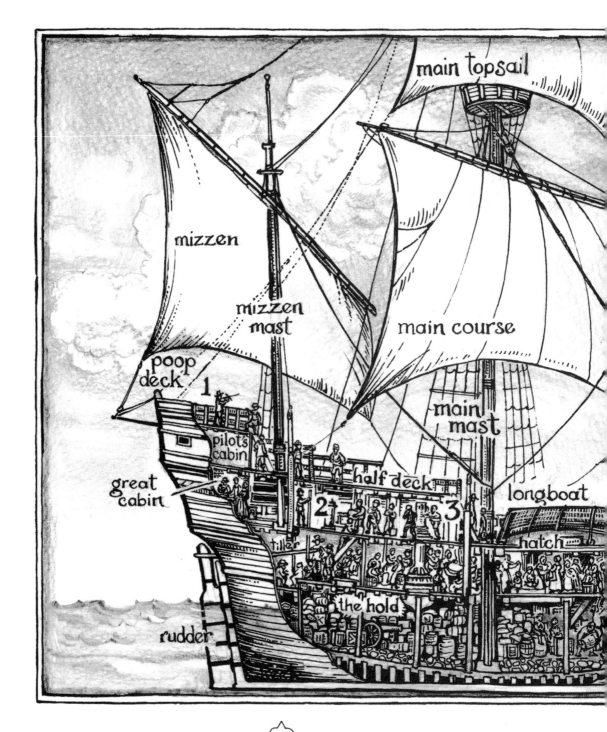

main topsail

mizzen

mizzen
mast

main course

poop
deck   1

main
mast

pilot's
cabin

half deck

longboat

great
cabin

2   3

hatch

tiller

the hold

rudder

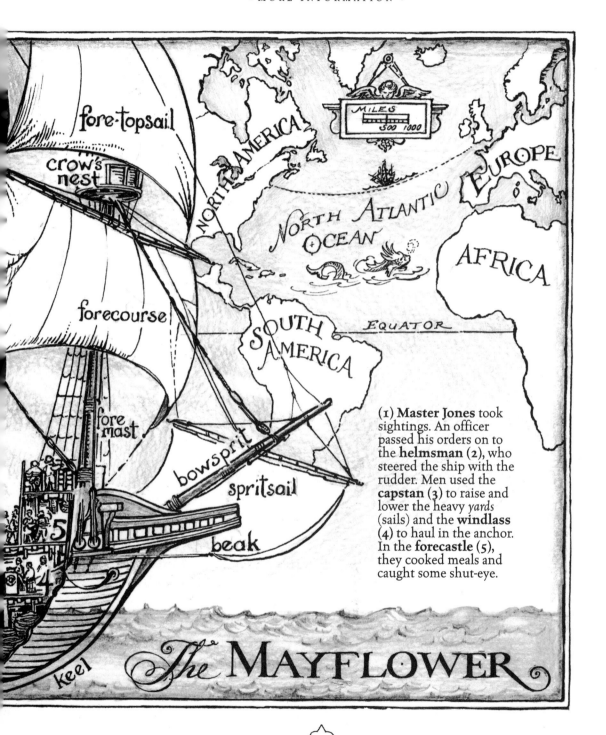

fore-topsail

crow's nest

NORTH AMERICA

MILES
500 1000

NORTH ATLANTIC OCEAN

EUROPE

AFRICA

forecourse

SOUTH AMERICA

EQUATOR

fore-mast

bowsprit

spritsail

beak

keel

(1) Master Jones took sightings. An officer passed his orders on to the **helmsman (2)**, who steered the ship with the rudder. Men used the **capstan (3)** to raise and lower the heavy *yards* (sails) and the **windlass (4)** to haul in the anchor. In the **forecastle (5)**, they cooked meals and caught some shut-eye.

The MAYFLOWER

Resources

BIBLIOGRAPHY

✳

Black, C. F., et. al. *Cultural Atlas of the Renaissance*. New York: Prentice Hall General Reference, 1993.

Bradford, William; Morrison, Samuel Eliot, editor. *Of Plymouth Plantation 1620–1647*. New York: Alfred A. Knopf, 1989.

Caffrey, Kate. *The Mayflower*. New York: Stein and Day, 1974.

Chitwood, Oliver Perry. *A History of Colonial America 1630–1776*. New York: Harper & Brothers, 1931.

Cumming, W. P., et al. *The Exploration of North America 1630-1776*. New York: G.P. Putnam's Sons, 1974.

Dersin, Denise, ed. et al. *What Life Was Like In the Realm of Elizabeth*. Alexandria, VA: Time-Life Books, 1998.

Dillon, Francis. *The Pilgrims, Their Journeys & Their World*. New York: Doubleday & Co., 1975.

Fleming, Thomas J. *One Small Candle, The Pilgrims' First Year in America*. New York: W. W. Norton & Co., 1963.

Grun, Bernard. *The Timetables of History*. New York: Simon & Schuster, 1979.

Harris, John. *Saga of the Pilgrims*. Chester, CT: The Globe Pequot Press, 1983.

Lerande, Jacques. *Chronicle of the World*. London: Longman Group UK Ltd., Chronicle Communications Ltd., 1989.

McEvedy, Colin. *The World History Factfinder*. New York: Gallery Books, 1984.

Purvis, Thomas L. *Colonial America to 1763*. New York: Facts on File, Inc., 1999.

Staff: Plimoth Plantation. *The Thanksgiving Primer*. Plymouth, MA: Plimoth Plantation Inc., 1987.

Trager, James. *The People's Chronology*. New York: Henry Holt & Co., 1992.

Viereck, Phillip. *The New Land*. New York: The John Day Company, 1967.

Willison, George F. *Saints and Strangers* New York: Reynal & Hitchcock, 1945.

RECOMMENDED FOR YOUNG READERS

✳

Anderson, Joan. Photos by George Ancona. *The First Thanksgiving Feast*. New York: Clarion Books, 1984.

Arenstam, Peter. et al. of Plimoth Plantation and Catherine O'Neill Grace. *Mayflower 1620*. Washington D. C.: National Geographic Society, 2003.

Clapp, Patricia. *Constance*. New York: Beech Tree Books, 1968.

Day, Nancy. *Your Travel Guide to Colonial America*. Minneapolis, MN: Runestone Press, 2001.

Goodman, Susan E. *Pilgrims of Plymouth*. Washington, D. C.: The National Geographic Society, 1999.

Harness, Cheryl. *Three Young Pilgrims*. New York: Simon & Schuster, 1992.

Kamma, Anne. Illus. by Bert Dodson. *If You Were At the First Thanksgiving*. New York: Scholastic Inc., 2001.

Mannis, Celeste Davidson. Illus. by Bagram Ibatoulline. *The Queen's Progress*. New York: Viking, 2003.

Waters, Kate. Photos by Russ Kendall. *Sarah Morton's Day*. New York: Scholastic Inc., 1989.

Yero, Judith Lloyd. *The Mayflower Compact*. Washington, D.C.: National Geographic Society, 2006.

PLACES WELL WORTH VISITING

Plimoth Plantation, 137 Warren Avenue (P. O. Box 1620), Plymouth, Massachusetts 02360   508.746.1622   www.plimoth.org

www.mayflowerhistory.com This is a swell, comprehensive Web site with loads of information
and images about life in colonial Massachusetts.

www.pilgrimhall.org not only tells you about Plymouth's Museum of Pilgrim Possessions, there are
lots of fine links as well, to all manner of Pilgrim information.

http://renaissance.dm.net/compendium and www.elizabethi.org
These two sites will give you plenty of information about the life and times of Queen Elizabeth I.

http://www.royal.gov.uk/output/Page75.asp is a fine introduction to King James I.

www.britannia.com/history has great timelines and plenty more.

THE PICTURES

The illustrations are done in pen and ink, my favorite way of doing artwork since I was 12 years old. Here's how I do them.
As I do my rough sketches, I'm surrounded by encyclopedia, illustrated chronologies, historical costume books, and
stacks of other books including those produced by Plimoth Plantation, the splendid living history museum at which the
staff and volunteers do their very best to show what life was like in southern New England in the 1620s. I pour over maps
and materials I gathered almost 15 years ago, when I was writing and illustrating my first historical picture book, *Three Young
Pilgrims*. Sure, plenty of imagination goes into drawing, but if I'm to honor these individuals back upstream in the living
past, the details must be accurate. When the sketches are done, I trace them onto watercolor paper or illustration board,
whichever is ready to hand, then I stick an old-fashioned steel pen point into a wooden holder. Again and again
I dipped this pen into a bottle of black ink to do the final line work. I erase away the pencil scribbles. Where more textures
and shadows are called for, I use pencil and black watercolor, a lot of one, a little of the other.

THE WORDS

As soon as I knew I was going to write this book, I did what I always do when beginning my research:
I went to my trusty set of World Books. After reading about Myles Standish and everything to do with his world, I set off to
the library. Among much that I found there were the words of Edward Winslow and Thomas Morton. Both gentlemen
are quoted briefly in these pages. But it was one particular book from my own library shelf which was by my side
throughout this writing: *Of Plymouth Plantation*, by William Bradford. In the 1989 edition that I used, which was edited and
very helpfully annotated by the historian, Samuel Eliot Morison, Bradford's 17th-century spelling has been modernized.
Nearly all of the quotations in my book are his. Any mistake in this book is mine.

My goal here, as in all of the books I have done and those that will be done, God willing, is a lively story
about those who are gone, faithful and true to their memory.

Index

To SPF, my congenial and indefatigable editor.

ACKNOWLEDGMENTS

Anyone who writes about the past must acknowledge the individuals, such as William Bradford, who took the time to record the happenings in his world. I'm grateful to them, to the folks at the reference desk at my library here in Independence, MO, and to the people of the living history museum, Plimoth Plantation.

Book design by David M. Seager. Design production by Ruthie Thompson, Thunderhill Graphics.
Text is set in Celestia Antiqua. Display type is Carmilla.

For information about special discounts for bulk purchases,
please contact National Geographic books Special Sales: ngspecsales@ngs.org.

Library of Congress Cataloging-in-Publication Data
Harness, Cheryl.
The adventurous life of Myles Standish and the amazing-but-true survival story of the
Plymouth Colony / written and illustrated by Cheryl Harness.
p. cm.
ISBN-10: 0-7922-5918-1; ISBN-13: 978-07922-5918- 3 (hardcover)
ISBN-10: 0-7922-5919-X; ISBN-13: 978-0-7922-5919-0 (library binding)
1. Standish, Myles, 1584?–1656—Juvenile literature. 2. Pilgrims (New Plymouth Colony)—Biography—Juvenile literature.
3. Massachusetts—History—New Plymouth, 1620–1691—Juvenile literature. I. Title.
F68.S825H37 2006
974.4'02092—dc22
2005031012

One of the world's largest nonprofit scientific and educational organizations, the National Geographic Society was founded in 1888 "for the increase and diffusion of geographic knowledge." Fulfilling this mission, the Society educates and inspires millions every day through its magazines, books, television programs, videos, maps and atlases, research grants, the National Geographic Bee, teacher workshops, and innovative classroom materials. The Society is supported through membership dues, charitable gifts, and income from the sale of its educational products. This support is vital to National Geographic's mission to increase global understanding and promote conservation of our planet through exploration, research, and education.

For more information, please call 1-800-NGS LINE (647-5463) or write to the following address:

NATIONAL GEOGRAPHIC SOCIETY
1145 17th Street N.W.
Washington, D.C. 20036-4688 U.S.A.
Visit the Society's Web site at www.nationalgeographic.com.

Printed in the United States of America